MW01632237

California's Historic Roadside Signs And Highway Markers

Alton Pryor

Stagecoach Publishing
5360 Campcreek Loop
Roseville, Ca. 95747
stagecoach@surewest.net

California Historic Roadside SIGNS and Highway Markers

ISBN: 978-0-692-88084-5

Stagecoach Publishing
5360 Campcreek Loop
Roseville, Ca. 95747
stagecoach@surewest.net

Throughout the centuries there were men who took first steps, down new roads, armed with nothing but their own vision.

Ayn Rand

Foreword

California's Mission Bell Markers

Mission Bell Marker

El Camino Real (The Royal Road) was California's Mission Trail.

The notion to preserve El Camino Real was first proposed by Miss Anna Pitcher in 1892. Miss Pitcher was director of the Pasadena Art Exhibition Association to the Women's Club of Los Angeles.

Anna Pitcher was unsuccessful in her bid.

She tried again in 1902. In this effort, she won the endorsement of the California Federation of Woman's Clubs and the Native Daughters of the Golden West.

Their mission was to mark the historical El Camino Real route with "bell" markers. Mrs. A.S.C. Forbes designed the historic bell that was first installed on an eleven-foot bent guidepost in front of the Old Plaza Church in downtown Los Angeles.

The Mission Bell Marker system has existed on the historic El Camino Real since 1906. The marker system originally intended to install a Mission Bell at one mile intervals on the El Camino Real highway.

By 1913, more than 450 markers were installed. Over the years, the bells were removed from the roadside for various reasons, including damage, vandalism, and theft.

In 1959, the Division of Highways was legislatively mandated to maintain the marker system.

The Mission Bell Marker consists of an 18-inch diameter cast metal bell set atop a 3-inch diameter pipe column attached to a reinforced concrete foundation using anchor rods.

Alameda County

No. 45: COLLEGE OF CALIFORNIA designates the site of the College of California on March 23, 1868. It was the forerunner of the University of California. The university moved from its Oakland site to its present site in Berkeley in 1873. A marker is at 13th and Franklin, Oakland.

No. 46: VALLEJO FLOUR MILL was built in 1856 by Jose de Jesus Vallejo, the brother of the General M.G. Vallejo. The stone aqueduct built to carry water to the mill parallels Niles Canyon Road. (Niles was once called "Vallejo Mills"). Vallejo Mills Historic Park is located on the northeast corner of Niles Canyon Road and Mission Boulevard (Highway 238), in Fremont.

No. 107: THE HOME OF JOAQUIN MILLER, called **"Poet** of the Sierras", wrote the poem, Columbus, among others. He built monuments dedicated to Moses, General John C. Fremont, and Robert Browning. He called his acreage "The Heights". It was purchased by the City of Oakland in 1919. A plaque exists at Joaquin Miller Park, Joaquin Miller Road and Sanborn Dr., Oakland.

No. 241: THE LIVERMORE MEMORIAL MONUMENT honors Robert Livermore, first settler of Livermore Valley. He was the first to engage in the planting of grapes, fruit and grain. A marker is located in Portola Park, Portola Ave. and N. Livermore Ave., Livermore.

No. 246: RANCHO SAN ANTONIO (Peralta Grant) was granted to Don Luis Maria Peralta by Governor Pablo de Sola for his forty years of service. The 43,000-acre land grant embraces the sites of the cities of San Leandro, Oakland, Alameda, Emeryville, Piedmont, Berkeley and Albany.

No. 279: THE ESTUDILLO HOME was built about 1850. Jose Joaquin Estudillo was the grantee of Rancho San Leandro. The family founded San Leandro, built a hotel and donated several lots, including the original site of San Leander's Church, to the city of San Leandro. A marker is located at 550 W. Estudillo Ave., San Leandro.

No. 285 PERALTA HOME was the first brick house built in Alameda County. It was built in 1860 for Ignacio Peralta, an early San Leandro Spanish settler. A marker is located at 561 Lafayette.

No. 299: CAMINO OF RANCHO SAN ANTONIO. It ran from Mission San Jose to Fruitvale, and later to San Pablo by way of Oakland and El Cerrito. Find the marker at corner of Oakland and Santa Clara avenues, Oakland.

No. 334: MISSION SAN JOSE. On June 9, 1797, troops led by Sergeant Pedro Amador, accompanied by Father Fermin Lasuen, set out for Santa Clara. They were seeking the spot the natives called Oroysom in the Valley of San Jose. A marker is located on Mission Blvd. at Washington Blvd., Fremont.

No. 335: THE SHELL MOUND was where Indians came to camp just above the shoreline. The Indians discarded the shells of their shellfish catches at the site. Eventually the shells covered hundreds of thousands of square feet. University of California excavated the site in the 1920s and found the mound consisted of clam, mussel and oyster shells. A marker is located in the 4600 block of Shell Mound St., Emeryville.

No. 440: ALAMEDA TERMINAL OF THE FIRST CONTINENTAL RAILROAD. It concentrated its activity from Sacramento to San Jose. A temporary connection was made at San Leandro with the San Francisco and Alameda Railroad. On September 6, 1869, the first Central Pacific train reached San Francisco Bay at Alameda. A marker is located at Naval Air Station Mall, Alameda.

No. 503: FIRST ALAMEDA COUNTY COURTHOUSE began construction June 6, 1853. The first court house and a marker are located at 30977 Union City Blvd. and Smith St., Union City.

No. 510: SAN FRANCISCO SOLANO ALVISO ADOBE. It was built in 1844-46 by Francisco Solano Alviso. It was originally called Alisal (the sycamores). During the battle of Sunol Canyon, General John C. Fremont used this building as his headquarters. A marker is located at 3459 Foothill Road, 3 miles south of Dublin.

No. 586: CRESTA BLANCA WINERY is where Charles A. Wetmore planted his vineyard in 1882. The Cresta Blanca wine won the highest honor at the 1889 Paris Exposition. A marker is located at 5050 Arroyo Road, Livermore.

No. 642: LELAND STANFORD WINERY. It was founded by Leland Stanford, U.S. Senator, and founder of Stanford University. To get to the marker from Highway 680, take Mission Blvd. to Stanford Ave. The winery is in Mission San Jose district, Fremont.

No. 676: SAINT MARY'S COLLEGE, often called the "Old Brick Pile", it survived from 1899 to 1928. A plaque was placed by Saint Mary's College alumni at 3093 Broadway and Hawthorne, Oakland.

No. 694: ST. JAMES THE APOSTLE CHURCH has given uninterrupted service since June 27, 1858. It, and its plaque are located at 1540 12th Ave. at Foothill Blvd, Oakland.

No. 768: FIRST SUCCESSFUL SUGAR BEET FACTORY was built by E.H. Dyer in 1870. It began processing sugar beets in 1870 and produced 293 tons of sugar during its first operating season. A marker is located at 30849 Dyer St. Union City.

No. 824: THE SAN LEANDRO OYSTER BEDS thrived during the 1890s, making it the most popular fishery in the state. Pollution has weakened the oyster industry in San Francisco Bay. The oyster beds and marker are located at the San Leandro Marina, south end of North Dike Road.

No. 849: MILLS HALL is the forerunner of Hue College. It transferred its operation from Benicia to Oakland in 1871. The college was once considered the most beautiful educational building in the state. The college provided homes for faculty and students as well as classrooms and dining halls. Its location is 5000 MacArthur at Pierson St., Oakland.

No. 884: THE PARAMOUNT THEATRE is an 'Art Deco' or 'Moderne' style of movie palace built during the rise of the motion picture industry. It opened December 16, 1931. It's marker is located at 2025 Broadway, Oakland.

No. 896: FIRST UNITARIAN CHURCH OF OAKLAND was designed by Walter J. Mathews. He departed from California's traditional Gothic wood frame construction. The church is noted for its world famous stained glass windows and for its arching redwood spans. A marker is at 685 14th Street at Castro Street, Oakland.

No. 908: THE BERKELEY CITY CLUB was organized by women in 1927 and built in 1929. The architect was Julia Morgan. Her interpretation of Moorish and Gothic elements created a landmark of California design. Find the marker at 2315 Durant Ave. Berkeley.

No. 925: THE PERALTA HACIENDA was built by Luis Peralta, one of California's earliest Spanish colonists. He received the largest Mexican land grant ever granted. His hacienda was the nucleus of the Rancho de San Antonio which covered the sites of seven present-day cities. It and a marker are at 2465 34th Ave. and Paxton St. Oakland.

No. 954: CROLL BUILDING was important in the Golden Age of Boxing. Jim Corbett and James Jeffries fought there. There is a marker at 1400 Webster Street, Alameda.

No. 957: THE WENTE BROTHERS WINERY introduced California's first varietal wine label, Sauvignon Blanc, in 1883. It is the oldest continuously operated family-owned winery in California. You'll find it and a marker at 5565 Tesla Road, in Livermore.

No. 962: THE BLOSSOM ROCK NAVIGATION TREE was used as a landmark to avoid striking the treacherous submerged Blossom Rock in San Francisco Bay. It and a marker are located in Redwood Regional Park, 11500 Skyline Blvd., Oakland.

No. 968: CHINA CLIPPER FLIGHT DEPARTURE was under the command of Captain Edwin C. Musick. The flight reached Manila, via Honolulu, Midway, Wake and Guam. See a marker in front of Building No. 1, Alameda Naval Air Station, Alameda.

No. 970: RAINBOW TROUT SPECIES was identified. The Rainbow Trout species was based on fish taken from the San Leandro Creek in 1885. The fishery is located in Redwood Regional Park, Oakland.

No. 986: PIEDMONT WAY was conceived in 1865 by Frederick Law Olmsted, America's foremost landscape architect. Olmstead envisioned a roadway that would follow the natural contours of the land and be sheltered from the sun and wind by an over-arching bowery of foliage. It's on Piedmont Avenue between Gayley Road and Dwight Way, Berkeley.

No. 1025: THE UKRANIA is the site of Agapius Honcharenko Farmstead. This is the burial site of the Ukranian patriot and exiled orthodox priest Agapius Honcharenko. He published the first American newspaper in Russian and Ukranian languages. A marker is located in Garin Regional Park, East Bay Regional Park District in San Francisco Bay.

No. 1929, THE USS HORNET, served in World War II and was known as the recovery ship for Apollo 11 and Apollo 12. It's at Pier 3 North, Alameda Point, 707 West Hornet Drive.

No. 1036: THE COAST GUARD LIGHTSHIP WLV 605. Lightships were floating lighthouses anchored in areas where it was too deep, expensive, or impractical to construct. Its marker is in Jack London Square, Oakland.

No. 641: THE CONCANNON VINEYARD was founded in 1883 by James Concannon. Grape cuttings from this vineyard were introduced to Mexico between 1889 and 1904. A marker is located at 4590 Tesla Rd., Livermore.

Alpine County

No. 240: MARKLEE'S CABIN SITE is where Jacob J. Marklee recorded 160 acres on June 23, 1862 in Douglas County, Nevada. After a boundary survey, it was determined the property was actually in California. The Alpine County Courthouse now occupies the site of Marklee's cabin.

No. 315: KIT CARSON marker stood on the summit of the Kit Carson Pass. Kit Carson inscribed his name on the Kit Carson Tree in 1844 when he guided Captain John C. Fremont over the Sierra Nevada. The original inscription was cut from the tree in 1888 and is now in Sutter's Fort, in Sacramento. The marker is located on State Highway 88, 14.5 miles W. of Woodfords.

No. 318: EBBETTS PASS ROUTE opened in the 1850s. The Emigrant Trail through Ebbetts Pass was discovered by Major John Ebbetts. A toll road, under the name of Carson Valley and Big Tree Road, helped open up the Comstock Lode in Nevada.

No. 378: MEMORIAL TO PIONEER ODD FELLOWS was where a group of pioneers inscribed their names and the emblem of the Independent Order of Odd Fellows on large rocks in 1849. A marker is located 14.4 miles west of Woodfords on State Highway 88.

No. 661: OLD EMIGRANT ROAD descended from its 9,460 foot summit to Placerville. It became obsolete in 1863.

No. 805: PONY EXPRESS REMOUNT STATION was located at Woodfords. It was here that Warren Upson scaled the mountains in a blinding snowstorm and down the eastern slope of the Sierra to Carson City. Five weeks later, the Pony Express was rerouted by way of Echo Summit and Luther Pass. A marker is located on Highway 89 State Highway 4 and Old Pony Express Road, Woodfords.

Amador County

No. 28: MAIDEN'S GRAVE. In 1850 a young girl named Rachel Melton accompanied her parents on a journey west in a covered wagon. She became violently ill. They camped and made every effort to cure her, but she died. She was buried on this spot. A marker is located on State Highway 88 miles west of Kirkwood.

No. 29: VOLCANO was discovered by Colonel Jonathan D. Stevenson's men, who mined Soldier's Gulch in 1849. At one time, Volcano had 17 hotels, a library, a theater, and courts of quick justice. During the Civil War, Volcano Blues smuggled the cannon, "Old Abe", in by hearse to quell rebels. A marker is Main and Consolation Sts., Volcano.

No 30: LANCHA PLANA (Flat Boat) was well-settled by 1850. The Amador Dispatch newspaper was born here in 1856. A marker is located on the north shore of Comanche Reservoir.

No. 31: DRYTOWN was founded in 1848. It is the oldest town and first in which gold was discovered in Amador County. The town was not dry, having once contained 26 saloons. See the marker located on Old State Highway 49.

No. 34: PIONEER HALL was organized by the Order of the Native Daughters of the Golden West September 11, 1886. A marker is located at 113 Main St., Jackson.

No. 35: Oleta (Old Fiddletown) was settled by Missourians in 1849. Fiddletown was a trading center for residents. The original Fiddletown name was restored. A marker is near Yee's Chinese Herb Shop;

No. 36: MIDDLE BAR was a gold rush town on the Mokelumne River. It's now covered by Pardee Reservoir.

No. 37: CLINTON was the center of a placer mining community in the 1850s and of quartz mining in the 1880s. The town once decided Amador County elections as its votes were always counted last. See the marker at E. Clinton and Clinton Blvd., Pine Grove.

No. 38: IRISHTOWN was an important stopping place for immigrants on their way to the Southern Mines. The first white settlers here found a "city of wigwams". A marker is located on Highway 88.

No. 39: BUTTE STORE is the only structure remaining of Butte City. It was a prosperous mining town during the 1850s. About 1854, Xavier Benoist ran and store and bakery in the building. It was later turned into a general merchandize store. Located on Highway 49.

No. 40: **KIRKWOODS** was built by Zack Kirkwood in 1864. When Alpine County was formed from Amador County, the division left the barn and milk house in Alpine County while the Alpine-El Dorado County line went directly through the bar room of the inn. It's on Highway 88.

No. 41: BIG BAR on the Mokelumne River was mined in 1848. The Whale Boat Ferry operated here until the bridge was built in 1852. A marker is on Highway 49.

No. 118: JACKSON GATE is on the north fork of Jackson Creek. It got its name from a fissure in a reef of rock that crosses the creek. In 1850, about 500 miners worked the area. The first mining ditch in the county was dug here. Its water sold for $1 per inch. A marker is located northeast of Jackson.

No. 322: SUTTER CREEK was named after John Sutter who was the first to mine the area in 1848. There was little activity until 1851 when quartz gold was discovered. It is located on Highway 49. A marker is at Veteran's Memorial Hall, Sutter Creek.

No. 470: PLYMOUTH TRADING POST is constructed entirely of brick and was built in 1857. In 1873 it became Plymouth Consolidated's new office and commissary. The marker is located on Main Street in Plymouth.

No. 506: THE COMMUNITY METHODIST CHURCH OF IONE was constructed locally fired brick and completed in 1866. It later was popularly known as the "Cathedral of the Mother Lode." There's a marker at 150 West Marlette, Ione.

No. 662: OLD EMIGRANT ROAD began a long loop around the Silver Lake Basin, reaching 9,640 feet in one place. The road was used by thousands of vehicles from 1848 to 1863. The marker is on Highway 88.

No. 715: FIRST AMATEUR ASTRONOMICAL OBSERVATORY is located in Volcano. It was built by George Madeira. It was here that Madeira discovered the Great Comet of 1861. A marker is located in Volcano.

No. 762: D'AGOSTINI WINERY was begun in 1856 by Adam Uhlinger, a Swiss immigrant. The original wine cellar had walls made from rock quarried from nearby hills. Some of its original vines are still in production. The marker is located on Shenandoah Road out of Plymouth.

No. 786: ARGONAUT AND KENNEDY MINES were discovered in 1850 and 1856 respectively. These mines played an important role in the economic development of California, producing $105,268,760 in gold. See the marker on Highway 49 north of Jackson.

No. 788 STEWART CO. STORE was built by Daniel Stewart in 1856. It was the first building erected in the Ione Valley. The town was once known as "Bedbug" and "Freeze Out". A marker is at 18 E. Main St. Ione.

No. 865: JACKSON'S PIONEER JEWISH SYNAGOGUE was dedicated September 18, 1857. High Holy Day worship continued until 1869. Its marker is located at Church and Main Streets, Jackson.

No. 867: PRESTON CASTLE was built in 1890-94. It is the most significant example of Romanesque Revival architecture in the Mother Lode. It was built to house the Preston School of Industry as an alternative to imprisoning juvenile offenders. Its marker is located in the town of Ione.

No. 1001: CALIFORNIA NATIVE AMERICAN CEREMONIAL ROUNDHOUSES CHAW SE' ROUNDHOUSE served as the center of ceremonial and social life. With its door facing the east, towards the rising sun, four large oaks are the focal point of this sixty-foot diameter structure. It's located at Chaw Se Indian Grinding Rock State Historic Park.

1007: KNIGHT FOUNDRY was established in 1873 to supply heavy equipment and repair facilities to the gold mines. A marker is located at 81 Eureka Street, Sutter Creek.

Butte County

NO. 313: HOOKER OAK was named by Annie E.K. Bidwell after English Botanist Sir Joseph Hooker. When the oak fell during a windstorm in 1977, it was estimated to be more than one thousand years old. It stood nearly 100 feet tall and measured 29 feet in circumference. The Hooker Oak marker is in Bidwell Park.

No. 314: OLD SUSPENSION BRIDGE was the first suspension bridge in California. The Mother Orange Tree of Butte County was planted here by Judge Joseph Lewis in 1856. This site is now covered by Oroville Reservoir.

No. 329: RANCHO CHICO AND BIDWELL ADOBE became the social and cultural center of the upper Sacramento Valley. The rancho included 26,000 acres. Rancho Chico was purchased by John Bidwell in 1845. In 1865 he began construction on the Bidwell Mansion. The mansion and a marker are located at Bidwell Mansion State Historic Park, 525 The Esplanade, Chico.

No. 330: BIDWELL'S BAR served as Butte County seat from 1853 to 1856. The site of the original courthouse is now under Lake Oroville 120 yards west of the road marker.

No. 770: CHINESE TEMPLE served as a worshiping site for 10,000 Chinese. Funds for its erection and furnishings were provided by the Emperor and Empress of China. Local Chinese labor built the structure. The marker is located at 1500 Broderick St., Oroville.

No. 771: DOGTOWN NUGGET DISCOVERY SITE is where the Dogtown Nugget weighing 54 pounds was discovered. A marker is at Pentz-Magalia Way, Magalia.

No. 807: OREGON CITY was established by a group of Oregonians who traveled over the Applegate and Lassen Trails. Shortly after, the party's captain, Peter Burnett, became the first civil Governor of California. You'll find a marker at Diggins Dr. between Oroville and Cherokee.

No. 809: ISHI, LAST YAHI INDIAN, and his family survived the Three Knolls Massacre. At one time the Yahi tribe numbered about 3,000 Indians. The remaining Yahi escaped but were forced into hiding. The monument is located at 2547 Oroville-Quincy Highway at Oak Ave, Oroville.

No. 840: CHICO FORESTRY STATION and nursery were established as an experimental forestry station. Its marker is at the Bidwell Nature Center, Cedar Grove and E. 8th Street, Chico.

No. 1043: MOTHER ORANGE TREE OF BUTTE COUNTY was a sweet orange seedling planted near the toll bridge at Bidwell's Bar. From this seedling a new industry sprouted hundreds of miles north of California's known citrus region. Its marker is located at 400 Glen Drive, Oroville.

Calaveras County

No. 41: BIG BAR is where miner's mined the Mokelumne River in 1848. The Whale Boat Ferry operated here until the first bridge was built in 1842. See its marker on High 49 at county line, four miles south of Jackson.

No. 251: VALLEY SPRINGS is where the San Joaquin and Sierra Nevada Railroad Company completed a narrow-gauge line. A marker is at intersection of Highways 12 and 26, Valley Springs.

No. 252: SAN ANDREAS was settled by Mexicans in 1848. It's named after the Catholic parish St. Andres. A newspaper was published here in 1846. Bandit Black Bart was tried here and sent to prison. A marker is located on Highway 49 and Main St.

No. 253: SANDY GULCH monument was erected in memory of pioneers of Sandy Gulch where William and Dan Carsner found large gold nuggets. See the marker on Highway 26, west of West Point.

No. 254: CAMANCHE was once called Limerick. It became Camanche (after Camanche, Iowa) in 1849. A fire destroyed Camanche's Chinatown in 1873. A marker is located at South Camanche Shore Park.

No. 255: CALAVERITAS was settled by Mexicans in 1849. The town was destroyed by fire in 1858. Its marker is 4.5 miles southeast of San Andreas.

No. 256: I.O.O.F. HALL at Mokelumne Hill is said to be the first three-story building erected outside the coastal towns. It was built in 1854 as a two-story building. A third story was added later.

No. 257: CAMP SECO was settled in 1849 by Mexicans who worked the placers in Oregon Gulch. The largest living cork oak tree in California was planted there in 1858. A marker is at Campo Seco and Penn Mine Rds. Campo Seco.

No. 258: FOURTH CROSSING, at Stockton-Murphys Road; crossed the Calaveras River. The town was once called "Foremans" and was a popular stage and freighting depot. Its marker is five miles south of San Andreas.

No. 261: CONGREGATIONAL CHURCH in Mokelumne was organized in 1853. The church is the oldest Congregational Church building in California. A marker can be seen at Main and Church Sts., Mokelumne Hill.

No. 262: MILTON was the completion site of the Southern Pacific Railroad in 1871. This marked the birth of the town named after Milton Latham, one of the railroad's construction engineers. A marker is located 15 miles north of Copperopolis.

No. 263: STONE CORRAL consists of a hotel, barns, and the large corrals for which it was named. Its marker is on Highway 26 southwest of Valley Springs.

No. 264: DOUBLE SPRINGS was founded in 1850. It was the county seat of Calaveras County. The old Courthouse was constructed of lumber brought from China and is still standing. Its marker is located on Double Springs Road 3.6 miles east of Valley Springs.

No. 265: CHILI GULCH was the richest placer mining section of Calaveras County. It received its name from Chileans who worked the area in 1848 and 1849. It was the scene of the so-called Chilean War. Its marker is on Highway 49, 1.4 miles south of Mokelumne Hill.

NO. 266 JENNY LIND is located on the north bank of the Calaveras River. It was a placer mining town as early as 1849. In 1864, half of its population of 400 was Chinese. You can see its marker on Milton Rd. 4.8 miles SW of Valley Springs.

No. 267: MITCHLER HOTEL was one of the oldest hotels still operating in California. It was first called the Sperry and Perry Hotel when it was opened by James L. Sperry and John Perry in 1856. It was later bought by College of the Pacific. A marker is at 457 Main Street in Murphys.

No. 268 WEST POINT was named by pioneer scout Kit Carson while looking for a pass over the Sierra. Author Bret Harte lived here for some time.

NO. 269: MOKELUMNE HILL was established by French trappers. Gold was discovered there in 1848. It was the center of the richest placer mining section of Calaveras County. The town was known for its bull and bear fights in 1854. A marker is at Main and Center Streets, Mokelumne Hill.

NO. 271: PIONEER CEMETERY was established in 1851. Most of its graves are unmarked. In 1936, stones appeared only on three of them. A marker is located 1.8 miles west of San Andreas.

No. 272 DOUGLAS FLAT was a roaring mining camp in early 1850. The Harper and Lone Star claims produced $130,000 in gold. A marker is located on Highway 4.

No. 273: VALLECITO was totally destroyed by fire August 28, 1859. Nearby is Moaning Cave, which Indians used as a burial ground. See the marker on Highway 4.

No. 274: Carson Hill was named after James H. Carson, who discovered gold there. In 1854, the largest gold nugget in California, weighing 195 pounds troy, was found. It marker is 3.7 miles south of Angels Camp.

No. 275: MURPHYS was named for a man who discovered gold on Murphys Flat in 1849. Murphys and surrounding towns produced $20,000,000 in gold. Early regulations restricted claims to 8 square feet. He marker is at Main and Jones Streets. Murphys.

No. 276: ROBINSON'S FERRY was established in 1848 by John W. Robinson and Stephen Mead to transport freight, animals and people across the river. Charges were 50 cents for each passenger, horse, jenny or other animal. It's 5.4 miles south of Angels Camp on Highway 49.

No. 280: GLENCOE (MOSQUITO GULCH) mines were first worked by Mexican miners in 1850. None of the town's buildings remain. A marker is located on Highway 26.

No. 281: O'BYRNE FERRY was a chain cable bridge opened in 1852. Some say this is the locale for Bret Harte's Poker Flat. Miners washed gold dust on both banks of the Stanislaus River here. The marker is on County Highway 48.

No. 282: EL DORADO was patented as a townsite in 1872. The town derived its name from a sawmill located there. A marker is at Mountain Ranch Rd. and Whiskey Slide Rd.

No. 284: JESUS MARIA was the center of a large placer mining section. It was named for a Mexican who grew vegetables and melons for the miners in the 1850s. Its marker is 4.9 miles southeast of Mokelumne Hill.

No. 286: RAILROAD FLAT was a historic mining town named after primitive mule-drawn ore-cars used in the mines. The Petticoat Mine was the largest producer. The town's population was decimated by "black fever" in 1880. A marker is at Railroad and Summit Level Rds., Railroad Flat.

No. 287: Angels Camp was founded by George Angel in 1849, who established a trading store and mining camp. It is famous as being the locale of Mark Twain's "The Jumping Frog of Calaveras County". There's a marker on Main St. and Birds Way, Angels Camp.

No. 288: ALTAVILLE has been the foundry town of Calaveras County. D.D. Demerest established a foundry there in 1854. A marker is at Highways 49 and 4, Altaville.

No. 295: PALOMA-GWIN MINE and Lower Rich Gulch were mined for placer gold in 1849. William M Gwin, California's first U.S. Senator, in 1851, acquired the property. It is located 5 miles east of Mokelumne Hill.

No. 296: COPPEROPOLIS is known for the copper discovered there in 1860. During the Civil War, and World Wars I and II the mines were the principal copper producing section of the U.S. A plaque is at the State Department of Forestry Station, Copperopolis.

No. 370: VALLECITO BELL MONUMENT is named for its bell, cast at Troy, New York in 1853. It was brought around the Horn. It was purchased from the ship with funds contributed by early-day residents and brought to Vallecito to be erected in a large oak tree in 1854. In 1859, a severe wind blew the tree down. See the marker at Church and Cemetery Lane, Vallecito.

No. 465: OLD MINING CAMP OF BROWNSVILLE thrived in the 1850s and1860s. It was named for Alfred Brown. Laws provided that each miner could own one wet, and one dry claim, not to exceed 150 square feet each. A marker is located 0.9 miles southwest of Murphys.

No. 466: THE PETER L. TRAVER BUILDING was built in 1856. It is the oldest stone building in the town of Murphys. Its iron shutters and sand on the roof protected it from fires in 1859, 1874 and 1893. Its marker is at 470 Main St., Murphys.

No, 499: RED BRICK GRAMMAR SCHOOL was built in 1848 with funds raised by a dance in the Billiard Saloon. It is one of the oldest schools in California. Its marker is at 125 N. Main St., Altaville.

No. 663: COURTHOUSE OF CALAVERAS COUNTY was built in 1852-1866. When the county seat was moved to San Andreas, George W. Leger acquired the court building and made it part of his adjoining hotel. It's located at Main and Lafayette, Mokelumne Hill.

No. 734: ANGELS HOTEL was first a canvas hotel built by C.C. Lake in 1851. It was replaced by a one-story wooden structure and then, in 1855, by one of stone. It's here that Samuel Clemens first heard the yarn that later brought him to fame as Mark Twain, author of the Jumping Frog of Calaveras County.

No. 735: PRINCE-GARIBARDI BUILDING was erected in 1852 by B.R. Prince and G. Garibardi for a general merchandise business. Its marker is at 298 S. Main Street, Altaville.

No. 769: BIRTHPLACE OF ARCHIE STEVENOT who was proclaimed "Mr. Mother Lode" in 1961 by the state legislature. Not only he, but his father and grandfather lent fame to the Carson Hill region of California.

No. 956: CALIFORNIA CAVERNS at Cave City is one of the earliest recorded official caves in the Mother Lode. Its marker is east of Highway 49 in San Andreas.

Colusa County

No. 238: SWIFT'S STONE CORRAL was built by Granville P. Swift in 1847. He and his partner, Frank Sears, needed a corral. There was no timber in the surrounding country so they built one of flat stones scattered nearby. It's located in Maxwell. A marker is located at Maxwell Sites Road, Maxwell.

No. 736: LETTS VALLEY was settled in 1855 by Jack and David Lett. The present lake spillway is the site of a tunnel they built to facilitate drainage. The brothers were killed in an effort to prevent squatters from settling on their land. A marker is at the Letts Lake Campground.

No. 890: COLUSA COUNTY COURTHOUSE was built in 1861 in a Federal/Classic Revival style. It is the oldest remaining courthouse in the Sacramento Valley. See the marker at 547 Market and Sixth Streets, Colusa.

Contra Costa County

No. 312: The John Muir Home is located in the city of Martinez at 4202 Alhambra Ave. The Muir Trail, Muir Woods National Monument and Muir Glacier in Alaska are all named for him. A plaque is at the John Muir National Historic Park, Martinez.

No. 356: CASTRO HOME, called the El Cerrito Adobe, was built near the northern bank of El Cerrito Creek. It was destroyed by fire in 1956. A marker if at 9800 San Pablo Ave., El Cerrito.

No. 455: DON FERNANDO PACHECO ADOBE was constructed in 1841 by Don Fernando Pacheco. It was reconstructed in 1941. A marker is at Grant and Solano Way, Concord.

No. 509: JOAQUIN MORAGA ADOBE was completed in 1841. Don Joaquin Moraga and his cousin, Don Juan Bernal, were awarded the Rancho Laguna de los Palos Colorados land grant in 1835. Don Joaquin was the grandson of Jose Joaquin Moraga, founder and first commandante of the Presidio of San Francisco.

No. 511: VICENTE MARTINEZ ADOBE was built on Rancho Pinole, which was granted to Martinez in 1836. It was later sold to Ed Franklin. A marker is located on Highway 4, Martinez.

No. 512: THE ALVARADO ADOBE was built in 1842 by Jesus Maria Castro for his mother, Dona Gabriela Berryessa de Castro. When she died, the adobe became the property of her daughter, Martina Castro de Alvarado.. See the marker at San Pablo Blvd. and Church Lane in San Pablo.

No. 515: DON SALVIO PACHECO ADOBE was built in in 1835. Don Salvio gave the land surrounding this adobe to refugees of the earthquake-flood of 1868. The community became known as Concord. A marker is at 1870 Adobe St., Concord.

No. 722: SITE OF THE MURDER OF DR. JOHN MARSH who practiced medicine from his home in Brentwood. While on his way home from Martinez on September 24, 1856, he was murdered by ruffians. A marker is at 4575 Pacheco, Blvd., Martinez.

No. 731: THE OLD HOMESTEAD was the first American home in Crockett. Its timbers have been well preserved. A marker is at 993 Loring Ave., Crockett.

No. 853: CAPTAIN PEDRO FAGES TRAIL is named for Fages who was the commandante at Monterey. In 1772, he searched for a way across San Francisco Bay. A marker is at 856 Danville Blvd., Danville.

No. 905: MOUNT DIABLO was a home with spiritual significance to the Costanoan Indians. A marker is at Mount Diablo State Park.

No. 932: MOUNT DIABLO COAL FIELD was the largest coal mining district in California from 1860-1914. There were five towns located near the coal fields: Nortonville, Somersville, Stewartsville, Judsonville and West Hartley. These towns are all gone. A marker is at Black Diamond Mines., Antioch.

No. 951: LIGHT STATIONS OF CALIFORNIA were built in the 1870s to provide both a light and roof signal to guide boats ferrying mail, passengers, and freight between San Francisco and various island ports.

No. 1002-1: GIANT POWDER COMPANY is the first company in America to produce dynamite. Following disastrous explosions at their San Francisco and Berkeley sites, the business moved to an isolated location at Point Pinole. A marker is at Grant and Atlas Roads, Richmond.

No. 1032: RICHMOND SHIPYARDS DISTRICT yards were constructed by Henry J. Kaiser in 1941 and 1942 for shipbuilding. In 1944, the yards were the largest in the world. A Marker is a 1040 Canal Blvd, Richmond.

Del Norte County

No. 497: S.S. EMIDIO was the first casualty of the Imperial Japanese Navy's submarine force action on the California coast. The ship was attacked some 200 miles north of San Francisco on December 20, 1941. Five crewmen died. The ship belonged to the General Petroleum Corporation. A marker is at Front and H Streets, Crescent City.

No. 541: BROTHER JONATHAN CEMETERY is dedicated to those who lost their lives in the wreck of the Pacific Mail Steamer Brother Jonathan. The wreck happened at point St. George Reef July 30, 1865. The marker is at Ninth Street and Pebble Beach Drive, Crescent City.

No. 544: FORT TER-WER was a U.S. military post established in 1857 by First Lieutenant George Crook to keep peace between the Indians and the whites. A marker is at Ter-Wer Riffle and Klamath Glen Roads, Klamath.

No. 545: CAMP LINCOLN was a U.S. military post established in 1862. It was built to keep peace between the Indians and the miners and settlers. A marker is on Kings Valley Road, Crescent City.

NO. 649: OLD INDIAN VILLAGE at Pebble Beach, Crescent City, was among the Tolowa Indian villages in northern Del Norte County. A arker is at 1886 Pebble Beach Dr., Crescent City.

No. 951: BATTERY POINT LIGHTHOUSE is one of the first lighthouses on the California coast. In 1885, Congress appropriated $15,000 for the construction of the light station. A marker is located at Battery Pt. Island, at the end of A Street, Crescent City.

El Dorado County

No. 141: HANGMAN'S TREE stood in the "Hay Yard". The stump is now under the building on which the Historic Marker is place at 305 Main St., Placerville.

No. 142: STUDEBAKER'S SHOP was built in 1850. It houses a blacksmith shop in front operated by Ollis and Hinds. John Mohler Studebaker made wheelbarrows for the gold miners. See the marker at 543 Main St., Placerville.

No. 143: MARSHALL MONUMENT commemorates James Marshall, who discovered gold in Coloma, causing the California gold rush. A marker is in Gold Discovery Park, Coloma.

No. 319: MARSHALL'S BLACKSMITH SHOP was purchased in 1887 to commemorate James Marshall, the discoverer of gold in California. The marker is located on Highway 193, Kelsey, CA.

No. 456: SHINGLE SPRINGS is where the Boston-Newton Joint Stock Association camped here in 1849. A marker is at Mother Lode Drive, near post office, Shingle Springs.

No. 475: OLD DRY DIGGINS-OLD HANGTOWN-PLACERVILLE was established on the banks of Hangtown Creek in 1848. A marker is at Bedford and Main, Placerville.

No. 484: Georgetown was founded in 1849 by George Phipps. It was once nicknamed "Growlersville" because of the heavy nuggets that "growled" in the miners' pans. A Marker is on Main Street in front of the fire station.

No. 486: EL DORADO MUD SPRINGS was originally a boggy mire caused by cattle and horses. It became the center of a mining district and the crossroads for freight and stage lines. A marker is at Pleasant Valley Road and Church Street, El Dorado.

No. 487: DIAMOND SPRINGS was settled in 1848. It derived its name from its crystal clear springs. A marker is at Highway 49 and China Garden Road, Diamond Springs.

No. 521: GREENWOOD is named for John Greenwood, a trapper and guide who came to California in 1844. He established a trading post in 1849. The marker is at Highway 193 and Greenwood St., Greenwood.

No. 530: GOLD DISCOVERY SITE includes John Sutter's saw mill where James Marshall discovered gold in the sawmill tailrace. A marker is located in Coloma.

No. 551: CALIFORNIA'S FIRST GRANGE HALL was called Pilot Hill Grange No. 1, with 29 charter members. A marker is on Highway 49, Pilot Hill.

No. 569: MORMON ISLAND is where three men, W. Sidney, S. Willis and Wilford Hudson, members of the Mormon Battalion, set out to hunt deer. They stopped on the south fork of the American River where they found gold. After telling their story when they returned to the fort, 150 Mormons and other miners flocked to the site. The site is now under Folsom Lake. A marker is at Folsom Point Picnic area.

No. 570: NEGRO HILL is another mining town that is now under Folsom Lake. Negro Hill is where pioneers whose graves were flooded with the lake were reburied. A marker is at Folsom Lake Recreation Area.

No. 571: SALMON FALLS. It's now under Folsom Lake. Marker is in Folsom Lake Recreation Area.

No. 572: CONDEMNED BAR is another site where graves that would be underneath Folsom Lake were reburied. See marker in Folsom Lake Recreation area.

Nos. 699: MORMON TAVERN-OVERLAND EXPRESS ROUTE IN CALIFORNIA. Pony Express rider Sam (Bill) Hamilton changed horses here. A plaque is just west of Clarksville.

No. 700: EL DORADO-NEVADA HOUSE (MUD SPRINGS) OVERLAND PONY EXPRESS ROUTE IN CALIFORNIA. See marker at Pleasant Valley Road, El Dorado.

No. 701: PLACERVILLE-OVERLAND PONY EXPRESS ROUTE IN CALIFORNIA. See marker on Main and Sacramento, Placerville.

No. 703: PLEASANT GROVE HOUSE OVERLAND PONY EXPRESS ROUTE. See marker on Green Valley Road, Rescue.

No. 704: SPORTSMAN'S HALL OVERLAND PONY EXPRESS ROUTE. See marker at 5622 Old Pony Express Trail, Cedar Grove.

No. 705: MOORE'S (RIVERTON) OVERLAND PONY EXPRESS ROUTE. See marker at U.S. Highway 50 and Ice House Road, Kyburz.

No. 706: WEBSSTER'S (SUGAR LOAF HOUSE OVERLAND PONY EXPRESS ROUTE. See marker on Highway 50, Kyburz.

No. 707: STRAWBERRY VALLEY HOUSE-OVERLAND PONY EXPRESS ROUTE. See marker at Strawberry.

No. 708: YANK'S STATION-OVERLAND PONY EXPRESS ROUTE. See marker on Highway 50 and Apache Ave., Meyers.

No. 728: FRIDAY'S STATION-OVERLAND PONY EXPRESS ROUTE. See marker at Stateline, Highway 50.

No. 747 COLOMA ROAD-RESCUE is where James W. Marshall carried the first gold discovered at Coloma. A marker is on Green Valley Rd., Rescue.

No. 748: COLOMA ROAD-COLOMA: James Marshall discovered gold in the tailrace of Sutter's sawmill. Thousands of miners used the road going to and from the diggings. A marker is at Marshall Gold Discovery Park.

No. 767: METHODIST EPISCOPAL CHURCH was built in 1851. It is the oldest church building in El Dorado County. See the marker at 1031 Thompson Way, Placerville.

No. 815: WAKAMATSU TEA AND SILK COLONY was a settlement of pioneer Japanese immigrants at Gold Hill on June 8, 1869. It was the only tea and silk farm established in California. It failed tragically in less than two years. A marker is at Gold Trails Elementary School, 889 Cold Springs Road, Gold Hill.

Fresno County

No. 344: ARROYO DE CANTUA was said to be the headquarters of notorious bandit Joaquin Murieta. He was supposedly killed here July 25, 1853 by a posse of state ranger led by Captain Harry Love. Plaques are located on Highway 198, Coalinga.

No, 488: FRESNO CITY gradually arose at the head of navigation of the Fresno Slough, and existed from approximately 1855 to 1875. Today there are no traces left. The City of Fresno was established some 30 miles to the southwest, on the newly build Central Pacific Railroad. A marker is in Tranquility.

No. 584: FORT MILLER now lies under the waters of Millerton Lake. A marker is at Millerton Lake State Recreation Area.

No. 803: FIRST JUNIOR COLLEGE in California was constructed in 1895. The school was known as Fresno High School from 1895 to 1921. It was established as the first junior college of California in 1910. It is the forerunner of Fresno State College. A marker is at Stanilaus and O Sts., Fresno.

No. 873: FRESNO FREE SPEECH FIGHT of the Industrial Workers of the World was held at the corner of Mariposa and I streets. See marker at Broadway and Mariposa Mall., Fresno.

No. 916: FORESTIERE UNDERGROUND GARDENS were created by Baldasare Forestiere in 1879. Excavating the hard pan by hand, he created a unique complex of underground rooms which rambled throughout a 10-acre parcel. A marker is at 5021 W. Shaw Street.

No. 934: TEMPORARY DETENTION CAMPS for Japanese Americans is dedicated to more than 5,000 Americans of Japanese ancestry who were confined at the Fresno Fairgrounds from May to October 1942. A marker is on the Fresno Fairgrounds.

Glenn County

No. 345: GRANVILLE P. SWIFT ADOBE was the site of Swift's cattle ranch where his droves of cattle were herded by Indian vaqueros. A marker is on Old Highway 99 at Hambright Creek, Orland.

No. 831: FIRST POSTED WATER NOTICE by Will S. Green, who arrived in San Francisco via Panama. Green was a ferryboat captain, mail carrier, surveyor, editor, writer, legislator, Surveyor General of the United States, and California State Treasurer. On December 18, 1883 on an oak tree he posted the first water notice stating that 500,000 miner's inches of river water was being diverted for irrigation of lands on the west side of the Sacramento Valley. A marker is at Cutler and First Aves., Hamilton City.

Humboldt County

No. 146: TRINIDAD HEAD was where Bruno de Hezeta, commandant of an expedition up the northwest coast, erected a cross and took possession in the name of Charles III of Spain. A marker is on Highway 101, Trinidad.

No. 154: FORT HUMBOLDT was built to protect both Indians and white settlers who were moving into the Humboldt Bay area. The fort was established in 1853. See a marker at 3431 Fort Ave., Eureka.

No. 164: OLD ARROW TREE was used by Indians to commemorate an important peace treaty. In memory of the treaty, each tribe, upon passing, was supposed to have shot an arrow into the bark. A marker is located at Korbel.

No. 173: CENTERVILLE BEACH CROSS marks the spot where the steamer Northerner, struck a hidden rock two miles off Cape Mendocino and drifted onto the Centerville beach. A marker is five miles west of Ferndale.

No. 215: CAMP CURTIS was headquarters of the Mountain Battalion from 1862 to 1865. There were many military posts established throughout the area to protect white settlers. It's located in Arcata.

No. 216: TOWN OF TRINIDAD was founded in 1850. Trinidad is the oldest town on the Northern California coast. During the 1850s, it served as a vital supply link between ships anchored at Trinidad Bay and miners in the Klamath, Trinity, Salmon River and Gold Bluff mines. A marker can be found at Edwards and Hector Sts., Trinidad.

No. 477: CITY OF EUREKA was founded in 1850 and is located on the remote northwestern coast. It was a major port of entry by water in the 19th century. A marker is Third and E Streets. Eureka.

No, 543: CALIFORNIA'S FIRST DRILLED OIL WELLS producing crude were located on the North Fork of the Mattole River. The Union Mattole Oil Company. A marker is on Mattole Rd and Front St., Petrolia.

No. 783: JACOBY BUILDING was built in 1857 for Augustus Jacoby. The building housed various mercantile firms during its early years. It was a refuge during times of Indian troubles. A marker is at Eighth and H streets, Arcata.

No. 838: OLD INDIAN VILLAGE OF TSURAI is a prehistoric Indian community. The houses were of hand-split redwood planks, designed for defense and protection. A marker is at SW corner of Ocean and Edward Sts., Trinidad.

No. 842: ARCATA AND MAD RIVER RAIL ROAD COMPANY was incorporated in 1854 as the Union Plank Walk, Rail Track, and Wharf Company. The Arcata and Mad River Rail Road is the oldest line on the north coast. It originally used a horse-drawn car. The railroad served as a link between Humboldt Bay and the Trinity River mines. See marker at 330 Railroad Ave., Blue Lake.

No. 882: HUMBOLDT HARBOR HISTORICAL DISTRICT is where Captain Jonathan Winship made the first recorded entry into Humboldt Bay. A marker is at Harold Larsen Vista Point, Eureka.

No. 883: FERNDALE was a pioneer agricultural community settled in 1852. It's long been known as "cream city" for its lasting contributions to the dairy industry. A marker is at Ferndale City Hall.

Imperial County

No. **182: TUMCO MINES** were discovered by Pete Walters of Ogilby. He found the first gold vein at Gold Rock on January 6, 1884. See marker on Gold Rack Ranch, Ogilby.

No. 193: PICACHO MINES were opened by placer miners in 1852. They expanded into hard-rock mining in 1895. Mill accidents, low quality ore and loss of cheap river transport and the building of Laguna Dam led to periods of inactivity. A marker is on Picacho R., Winterhaven.

No. 194: MOUNTAIN SPRINGS STATION is where Peter Larkin and Joe Standiff operated a store from a stone house. Ox teams pulled wagons up a 30 percent grade. It was used as toll road until 1876. A plaque is adjacent to Desert View Tower.

No. 350: MISSION LA PURISMIMA CONCEPTION is where Father Francisco Garces began a mission. The mission was poorly supported. Frustrated and disheartened, the Quechans (Yumas) destroyed Concepcion. A marker is on Picacho Rort, Fort Yuma.

No. 568: Hernando de Alarcon Expedition was to provide supplies for Francisco Coronado's expedition in search of the fabled Seven Cities of Cibola. See the marker at All-American Canal.

No. 806: FORT YUMA was originally called Camp Calhoun. A fire destroyed the original buildings. It was called Fort Yuma in 1852. A marker is on the bank of the Colorado River, 350 Picacho Rd., Winterhaven.

No. 808: CAMP SALVATION was established in 1849 by Lieut. Cave J. Couts, Escort Commander, Internation Boundary Commission. It served as a refugee center for distressed immigrants attempting to reach the gold fields.

No. 845: OLD PLANK ROAD was seven miles long and the only means early motorists had of crossing the treacherous Imperial sand dunes. The 8-by-12-foot sections were moved with a team of horses whenever the shifting sands covered portions of the road. The plank road is 18 miles west of Winterhaven. Marker is at Grays Well Road, Winterhaven.

No. 921: MISSION SAN PEDRO Y SAN PABLO DE BICUNER was a pueblo founded by Spanish missionaries in 1781. A marker is on Levee and Mehring Rds., Bard.

No. 939: TWENTIETH CENTURY FOLK ART ENVIRONMENT was also known as Charley's World of Lost Art. Charles Kasling began sculpturing near Andrade in 1967. His creations now fill a site of about two and a half acre. A marker is five miles north of Andrade, Winterhaven.

No. 944: FORT ROMUALDO PACHECO opened an overland route from Sonora to California in 1774. It was the only Mexican fort in Alta California. A marker is on the bank of the New River, Imperial.

No. 985: DESERT TRAINING CENTER was established by General George C. Patton, Jr. Camp Pilot Knob was a unit of the training center which was built to prepare troops for battle during World War II. It was the largest military training ground ever to exist. A marker is located on Sidewinder Road, town of Felicity.

No. 1008: YUHA WELL is also known as Santa Rosa de Las Lajas (Flat Rocks). This site was used by the Anza Exploring Expedition, opening the land route from Sonora, Mexico to Alta California. A marker is at the Eastbound Sunbeam Roadside Rest Area.

No. 1034: TECOLOTE RANCHO was the Imperial Valley home of Harold Bell Wright author of "The Winning of Barbara Worth". He built the Rancho Tecolote while living in a tent. A marker is on East Country Highway 8 and Barbara Worth Rd., Holtville.

Inyo County

No. 208: SAN FRANCIS RANCH was established by Samuel A. Bishop. In 1861, Bishop left Fort Tejon driving 650 head of cattle to the Owens Valley. He stopped at a creek, later named for him, and established San Francis Ranch. A marker is on Red Hill Rd. and State Highway 168.

No. 209: BEND CITY was a population center in the mid-1860s. It was the county seat of Coso County, but the county was never formed. The first bridge across the Owens River was built here, but an earthquake changed the course of the Owens River. The town was left sitting on an empty ravine. A marker is on Mazourka Canyon Rd., Independence.

No. 211: MAYFIELD BATTLE GROUND was the scene where on April 8, 1862, a body of troopers and settlers entered Mayfield Canyon intending to do battle with Indians. The Indians never showed. A marker is on Pine Creek Road and North Round Valley Road., Bishop.

No. 223: PUTNAM'S CABIN was built in 1861 and used as a permanent home, a trading post, hospital, and a fort for early settlers. The settlement of Putnam was changed five years later to Independence. A marker is at 139 Edwards St., Independence.

No. 229: MARY AUSTIN'S HOME is where she wrote "The Land of Little Rain" and other novels. The home and marker are located 253 Market St., Independence.

No. 230: FIRST PERMANENT WHITE HABITATION in the Owens Valley occurred when three men drove their cattle there and prepared to stay. A marker is at the intersection of State Highway 6 and Silver Canyon Road., Bishop.

No. 349: CAMP INDEPENDENCE FORT was built at the request of settlers. Colonel George Evans led a military expedition to the site that is now called Independence. A marker is on Miller Lane and Salvabell Lane, Indepenence.

No. 441: BURNED WAGONS POINT was the location where gold seekers from the Midwest entered Death Valley seeking a short route to California. A marker is located at Death Valley National Monument, Stovepipe Wells.

No. 442: DEATH VALLEY GATEWAY was a natural path 49ers took in seeking a shortcut to California's gold fields. A marker is at Death Valley National Monument Stovepipe Wells.

No. 443: VALLEY WELLS is where several groups of emigrants sought to secure water after escaping from the harsh conditions of Death Valley. A marker is at Trona Wildrose Road at Valley Wells Rd., Trona.

No. 444: BENNETT-ARCANE LONG CAMP is where migrants were stranded for a month and almost died from starvation. Two men, William Lewis Manley and John Rogers made a heroic journey to San Fernando on foot, returning with supplies. A marker is at intersection of Badwater Rd., and Westside Rd.

No. 507: GRAVE OF 1872 EARQUAKE VICTIMS. A major earthquake shook the Owens Valley in 1872, destroying the town of Lone Pine and killing 14 or more people. They were buried in a mass grave north of Lone Pine.

No. 537: COTTONWOOD CHARCOAL KILNS. These kilns were used to turn wood into charcoal. After turning the wood into charcoal it was loaded aboard the steamer Bessie Brady and hauled across the lake to the Cerro Gordo mine.

No. 752: FURNACE OF OWENS LAKE LEAD COMPANY was built by Colonel Sherman Stevens in 1869 and used until 1874. A marker is on State Highway 136 near the town of Keeler.

No. 773: OLD HARMONY BORAX WORKS. In 1881 Aaron Winters discovered borax on a marsh. The work of gathering the ore (called cottonball was done by Chinese workmen. A marker is at Death Valley National Monument.

No. 796: FARLEY'S OLANCHA MILL. In 1860, M.H. Farley worked for the Silver Mountain Mining Company in the Coso Mountains. He got the idea of building a processing mill on a creek that flowed into Owens Lake. He completed the mill and furnace in 1862. A marker is on State Highway 395 at Fall Road, Olancha.

No. 811: BISHOP CREEK BATTLEGROUND. In 1862, a battle took place at this site between newly arrived emigrants to Owens Valley and the Paiute and Shoshone Indians. A marker is on State Highway 168 and Bishop Creek Road, Bishop.

No. 826: OLD STOVEPIPE WELLS. This waterhole was the only one in the sand dune area of Death Valley. When sand obscured the spot, a length of stovepipe was inserted as a marker.

No. 848: EICHBAUM TOLL ROAD. In 1926, H.W. Eichbaum obtained a franchise for a toll road from Darwin Falls to Stovepipe Wells. It was the first maintained road into Death Valley from the West. A plaque is at Death Valley National Monument, Stovepipe Wells.

No. 850: MANZANAR RELOCATION CENTER. In the early part of World War II, persons of Japanese ancestry were interned in relocation centers. Manzanar confined 10,000 persons, the majority of them American citizens. A marker is 9.6 miles North of Lone Pine.

No. 953: LAWS NARROW GUAGE RAILROAD STATION. The Carson & Colorado Railroad was built in 1883. It ran from Mound House, near Carson City, Nevada, through Laws and Keeler, California. A marker I s on Silver Canyon Rd., Bishop.

Kern County

No. 97: OAK CREEK PASS. In 1776, Father Francisco Garces used the Oak Creek Pass to return to Mojave after exploring the San Joaquin Valley. A marker is on Willow Pass Rd., Tehachapi.

No. 98: KEYSVILLE was a center of both placer and quartz gold mining. On a knoll just below the townsite are the outlines of an earthworks fort, built to meet a possible Indian attack. A marker is on Black Gulch Rd., Lake Isabella.

No. 99: WALKER'S PASS was discovered by Joseph R Walker, an American trailblazer. He left the San Joaquin Valley through this pass in 1834. A marker is at the summit of State Highway 178.

No. 100: HAVILAH. Gold deposits were found here in 1864. Havilah was the county seat between 1866, when Kern County was organized, and 1872, when the government was moved to Bakersfield. State plaque is in front of Bodfish post office.

No. 129: FORT TEJON was a military post established in 1854. Its purpose was to suppress livestock rustling. The fort was abandoned in 1864. A marker is at Fort Tejon State Park.

No. 130: **WILLOW SPRINGS** was visited by Padre Garces in 1776 while following the old Horse Thief Trail (later known as the Joe Walker Trail). The famished Jayhawk Party of 1850 found water here while struggling from Death Valley to Los Angeles. A marker is on Manly Rd., Rosamond.

No. 132: KERNVILLE was called Whiskey Flat until 1864. Kernville was founded in 1860 when whiskey dealer Adam Hamilton moved shop there. "Lovely" Rogers found the "Big Blue Ledge" while tracking a stray mule. A marker is at Old Kernville Cemetery, Kernville.

No. 133: SEBASTIAN INDIAN RESERVATION was established in 1853 by General Edward Fitzgerald Beale as one of several in California. General Beale acquired title to the property under a Mexican Land Grant in 1843. A marker is on Grapevine Rd. and D. Street, Mettler.

No. 137: GORDON'S FERRY was an over-head cable type ferry across the Kern River. An Adobe station house also served as a station for the Butterfield Overland Mail. See a marker at Kern River Bridge, Bakersfield.

No. 277: GARCES CIRCLE is the approximate site of the Indian Rancheria visited by Padre Francisco Garces in 1776. Padre Garces named the spot *San Miguel de los Noches por el Santa Principe.* A marker is on intersection of Chester Ave. and 30th., Bakersfield.

No. 278: PLACE WHERE FRANCISCAN GARCES CROSSED THE KERN RIVER. Franciscan friar Francisco Garces crossed the Kern River searching for a shorter route from Sonora, Mexico to Monterey, California. A marker is at Rancheria Road, Bakersfield.

No. 283: GRAPEVINE PASS. Don Pedro Fages passed this site while traveling from San Diego to San Luis Obispo. A marker is on Lebec Road, Lebec.

No. 290: DISCOVERY WELL of the Kern River Oilfield was discovered at 70 feet in 1899. On June 1, 1899, Horace and Milton McWhorter drilled the regions first commercial well. A plaque is on Round Mountain Road, Bakersfield.

No. 291: FAGES-ZALVIDEA CROSSING. In 1772, Don Pedro Fages crossed here on his way from San Diego to San Luis Obispo. A marker is on State Highway 166, Mettler.

No. 300: ROSE STATION was a vaquero camp of the Sebastian Indian Reservation. William B. Rose built an adobe stage station here. A marker is on Grapevine Road and D Street, Mettler.

No, 371: OUTERMOST POINT in the South San Joaquin Valley visited by Padre Garces in 1776. Garces was seeking a route from Mexico to California. A marker is in the courtyard of Saint Thomas the Apostle Church., Arvin.

No. 374: TULAMNIU INDIAN SITE was a Yokuts village of Tulamniu. This village was occupied for several centuries, and in 1933-34 was excavated by the Smithsonian Institution. A marker is at the pumping station east of Taft.

No. 376: CALIFORNIA STANDARD oil well Number 1 was one of the early wells that in 1899 started a new oil field called the McKittrick Field. A marker is at McKittrick Field, McKittrick.

No. 382: COLONEL THOMAS BAKER memorial honors a man who was a friend to all travelers. Bakersfield was named for custom of teamsters who, when asked where they had stayed the previous night, replied "Baker's Field". A marker is at City Hall, Bakersfield.

No. 457: INDIAN WELLS is where the Manly-Jayhawker parties of 1849 found their first water on the Joseph R. Walker Trail. During the 1860s, it was the site of a stage and freight station. A marker is at Indian Wells Lodge.

No. 476: DESERT SPRING was on an old Indian horse thief trail. The famished Manly-Jayhawk Death Valley parties were revived here after coming through Indian Wells and Last Chance Canyon. A marker is at the Corner of Pappas Ranch. Cantil.

No. 485: LAKEVIEW GUSHER 1. America's most spectacular gusher blew here March 14, 1910. A marker is on Petroleum Club Road, Maricopa.

No. 492: BUTTONWILLOW TREE. This lone tree gave the town of Buttonwillow its name. It was the site of Miller and Lux's headquarters. A plaque is on Buttonwillow Dr., Buttonwillow.

No. 495: GLENNVILLE ADOBE. This is Kern County's oldest residence. A plaque is at the Kern Co. Fire Dept., Glennville.

No. 498: MCKITTRICK BREA PIT. This was an ancient asphaltum seepage in which birds and animals became trapped. A marker is at State Highway 33 and State Highway 58, McKittrick.

No. 504: BUENA VISTA REFINERY. California's first oil refineries were built here. A marker is on Highway 33 and LoKern Rd., McKittrick.

No. 508; TEHACHAPI LOOP. A 4,000 foot train will cross 77 feet above its rear cars in the tunnel below. Marker is at corner of Bakersfield-Glennville Rd. Bakersfield.

No. 539: POSEY STATION OF BUTTERFIELD OVERLAND MAIL LINES. The line ran from St. Louis, Missouri through Kern County to San Francisco. A marker is at Bakersfield-Glennville Rd, Bakersfield.

No. 540: SINKS OF THE TEJON, ALSO KNOWN AS ALAMO, STATION OF THE BUTTERFIELD OVERLAND MAIL. This stage line operated in Kern County during 1858-61. A marker is on David and Wheeler Ridge Rds., Mettler.

No. 581: WELL, 2-6. This well blew over the top of the derrick and produced 2,000 barrels per day. A marker is at Fellows Fire Station, Fellows.

No. 588. KERN RIVER SLOUGH STATION. This was a Butterfield Stage station. A markere is on Panama Road, Lamont.

No. 589: MOUNTAIN HOUSE. This was a Butterfield Stage Station. A marker is at Dry Creek, Woody.

No. 631: GARCES BAPTISMAL SITE. This was the site of the first recorded Christian baptism in the San Joaquin Valley. A marker is on State Highway 155, Woody.

No. 643: OLD TOWN (TEHACHAPI). This is the oldest settlement in Tehachapi Valley. A marker is Old Town Road and Woodford-Tehachapi Rd., Tehachapi.

No. 652: TWENTY MULE TEAM BORAX TERMINUS. The ore wagons were built in Mojave at a cost of $900 each. A marker is located at 16246 Sierra Highway, Mojave.

No. 660: POINT ON THE JEDEDIAH SMITH TRAIL. Jedediah Smith passed through here with a party of fur trappers. A marker is Old Bena and Tower Line Roads, Edison.

No, 671: SITE OF TOWN OF GARLOCK. In 1896, Eugene Garlock built a stamp mill here to crush gold ore from the Yellow Aster Mine on Rand Mountain. A marker is at State Highway 395 on Garlock Road., Cantil post office.

No. 672: LAVERS CROSSING. John C. Reid filed a squatters claim here in 1854. In 1859, David Lavers and his son built a hotel and stage barn. A marker is on the corner of White River and Jack Ranch Roads., Glennville.

No. 690: SITE OF THE LAST HOME OF ALEXIX GODEY. Godey was frontiersman and scout. He was a guide at one time for John C. Fremont. A marker is at 414 Nineteenth St., Bakersfield.

No. 732: SITE OF THE HOME OF ELISHA STEVENS. Stevens was a pathfinder and scout for he Murphy-Townsend party. A marker is at W.Columbus and Isla Verde Sts., Bakersfield.

No. 741: BEALVILLE. Edward Fitzgerald Beale established a home on Rancho le Libre in 185. A marker is on Bealville Rd and State Highway 58, Caliente.

No. 742: CAPSITE OF EDWARD M KERN. John C. Fremont named the river in honor of Edward M. Kern. A marker is posted at the entrance to Old Isabella Rd. Recreation Area., Lake Isabella.

No. 757: CALIENTE. Originally known as Allen's Camp, the settlement was named Caliente when railroad construction reached here. A marker is at Bealville Rd., Caliente.

No. 766: FREEMAN'S JUNCTION. Explorer Joseph R. Walker passed this junction of Indian trails while discovering Walker Pass. A marker is on Highway 178 of junction with State Highway 14.

No. 923: SITE OF THE FLIGHT OF THE GOSSAMERE CONDOR. A plaque at Shafter Airport, commemorates the world's first man-powered flight to complete the Kremer Circuit.

No, 938 RAND MINING DISTRICT. When the Rand Mine, also known as the Yellow Aster, was discovered, the town of Randsburg soon followed. A marker is at the Kern Co. Deseret Museum, Butte Ave., Randsburg.

Kings County

No. 206: EL ADOBE DE LOS ROBLES RANCHO. The restored adobe is the second oldest in the San Joaquin Valley. It was built by Daniel Rhodes, who came to California in 1846 by overland caravan. He and his brother John were among the first expedition that attempted to rescue the Donner Party. A marker is at 10036-19 1/2 Ave. and Lacy Blvd., Lemoore.

No. 245: SITE OF MUSSEL SLOUGH TRAGEDY. There was a dispute over land titles between settlers and the railroad. A fight broke out in which two U.S. Marshalls and five ranchers lost their lives. The legal struggle over titles was finally settled by compromise.

No. 270: KINGSTON. The town was founded in 1856 by L.A. Whitmore, who operated the first ferry to cross the Kings River. Kingston became a stopping place for Butterfield stages after 1858. On December 26, 1873, Tiburcio Vasquez and his gang robbed the entire town.

Lake County

No. 426: STONE AND KELSEY HOME: This home was built by Charles Stone and Andy Kelsey on land purchased from Salvador Vallejo. They forced Indians to do the construction work, causing resentment. In 1849, the Indians killed both Stone and Kelsey. A marker located at Main and Bell Hill Road, Kelseyville.

No. 427: BATTLE OF BLOODY ISLAND: U.S. soldiers nearly annihilated the Indian inhabitants for the murder of two white men, Charles Stone and Andrew Kelsey. Doubt exists about the Indians' guilt. A marker is located at the intersection of State Highway 20 and Reclamation Rd. Upper Lake.

No. 428: SULPHER BANK MINE became one of the most noted quicksilver producers in the world in1865. In four years, it produced 2,000,000 pounds of quicksilver. A marker is 1.5 miles south of Clearlake Oaks.

No. 429: LOWER LAKE STONE JAIL. This jail was claimed to be the smallest in the United States. It was erected in 1876 of stone locally quarried and reinforced with iron. A marker is at Highway 29 and Hidden Valley R:oad, Lower Lake.

No. 450: STONE HOUSE is the oldest building in Lake County. It was built in 1853-54 by Robert Sterling, whose wife was the first non-Indian woman in Coyote Valley. It was built in 1894 and served as headquarters of the Gueroc land grant and the first store in the valley. A marker is at Highway 29 and Hidden Valley Road, Middletown.

No. 467: HELENA TOLL ROAD AND BULL TRAIL was built by volunteers in the 1850s. It was an official road in 1861 but abandoned in 1868. A number of grades were 35 percent. A marker is on State Highway 29 and Hill Ave., Middletown.

No. 897: OLD LAKE COUNTY COURTHOUSE. This brick and mortar courthouse was constructed in 1870-71 by A.P. Pettit. It was one of the few buildings to survive the 1906 earthquake. Precedent-setting trials on water rights were held here. A marker is at 255 N. Main St., Lakeport.

Lassen County

No. 76: ROOP'S FORT was built in 1854 by Isaac N. Roop as a stopping place for emigrant trains. It became the locale for the "sagebrush" war, fought in 1863. A marker is at Memorial Park, Susanville.

No. 565: PETER LASSEN GRAVE marks the site where Peter Lassen was killed by Indians April 27, 1859. A marker is at 2550 Wingfield Rd., Susanville.

No. 675: NOBLE EMIGRANT TRAIL SUSANVILLE: This was previously a meadow and is now a park and was once a stopping place for emigrants. A marker is in Lassen Memorial Park, Susanville.

No. 677: NOBLE EMIGRANT TRAIL: This route was first used in 1852 by emigrants seeking to avoid the hardships of the Lassen Trail. A maker is on Highway 395 north of Litchfield.

No. 678: LASSEN EMIGRANT TRAIL. Many covered wagons passed through this draw enroute to California. The trail passed the Bogard Ranger Station and proceeded southward to Big Springs and Big Meadow (now Lake Almanor) A marker is on Highway 36, west of Westwood.

No. 758: FORT JANESVILLE. The people at Honey Lake were terrified by the Ormsby Massacre. They built a stockade for protection from another Indian Attack which never occurred. A marker is on Main St., Janesville.

No. 763: LASSEN EMIGRANT TRAIL, BIEBER. Peter Lassen opened this emigrant trail in 1848 when he led a 12-wagon emigrant train from Missouri to California. Because of the hardships of the trail and the hostility of Indians, the trail was little used after 1853. A marker is at County of Lassen Library Historical Museum, Bieber.

Los Angeles County

No. 127: CASA DE GOVERNOR PIO PICO. Following the Mexican War, Pio Pico, the last Mexican governor, acquired the 9,000-acre Rancho Paso de Bartolo. He built an adobe home that was destroyed by floods in 1883-84. His second adobe casa, now known as the Pio Pico Mansion, represents both Mexican and American cultures. A marker is at 6003 Pioneer Blvd. Whittier.

No. 144: NUESTRA SENORA LA REINA LOS ANGELES. Translated it means, "The Church of Our Lady the Queen of the Angels". It was the only church for the pueblo. Today, it serves the Hispanic population of Los Angeles. A marker is at 535 N. Main Street.

No. 145: AVILA ADOBE was built in 1818 by Don Francisco Avila, alcalde (mayor) of Los Angeles. It is the oldest existing house in Los Angeles. A marker is on Olvera Street, Los Angeles.

No. 147: BANNING PARK is named for General Phineas Banning. He was a state senator and pioneer in the development of transportation in Southern California. He died in 1885. In 1927, his property at 401 East M Street, Wilmington, was deeded to the city. A marker is at 401 East M Street, Wilmington.

No. 150: BRAND PARK (Memory Garden) is part of the original land grant of Mission San Fernando de Rey de Espana. You'll find a marker located at 15174 San Fernando Mission Blvd., Los Angeles.

No. 151: CAMP DE CAHUENGA. It was here that the Treaty of Cahuenga was made by General Andres Pico and Lieutenant-Colonel John C. Fremont. The treaty, signed January 13, 1847, allowed the United States to acquire California. A marker is located at 3919 Lankershim Blvd, North Hollywood.

No. 152: DOMINGUEZ RANCHHOUSE. The central portion of the ranch house was built in 1826 by Manuel Dominguez. Rancho San Pedro contains 10 square leagues of land and was granted by Governor Fages to Juan Jose Dominguez in 1874. It was re-granted by Governor Sola to Cristobal Dominguez in 1822. A marker is at 18127 Alameda, Compton.

No. 156: LOS ANGELES PLAZA. This was part of the original pueblo lands of *El Pueblo de la Reina de Loa Angeles de Porciuncula* founded in 1781. A marker is in the 500 block of N. Main, Los Angeles.

No. 157: MISSION SAN FERNANDO REY DE ESPANA. The mission was founded by Father Lasuen September 8, 1797. An adobe chapel was built in 1806, but was heavily damaged by the destructive earthquake of 1812. A new church was completed in 1818. A marker is located at 15151 San Fernando Mission Blvd., Mission Hills.

No. 158: MISSION SAN GABRIEL ARCANGEL. The mission was founded September 8, 1771 by Padres Pedro Benito Cambon and Angel Fernandez de la Somera. A marker is at 537 W. Mission Blvd., San Gabriel.

No. 159: PICO HOUSE (Hotel). Pio Pico constructed the Pio Pico House in 1869-70. It was the first three-story hotel built in Los AngelesA marker is in the 400 Block of Main Street, Los Angeles.

No. 160: PLUMMER PARK AND OLDEST HOUSE IN HOLLYWOOD. The house was built in the 1870s by Eugene Raphael Plummer. See the marker at 23537 Calabasas Rd., Calabasas.

No. 161: MISSION VIEJA was the name given the first buildings erected and later abandoned by the fathers for Mission San Gabriel Archangel. A marker is at San Gabriel and N. Lincoln Ave., Montebello.

No. 167: LA MESA BATTLEFIELD. This battlefield served as a campsite for the California forces under General Jose Maria Castro in the summer of 1846. The Battle of La Mesa was fought January 9, 1847. A marker is located 4490 Exchange Ave., Vernon.

No. 168: OAK OF THE GOLDEN DREAM was the site where Francisco Lopez made California's first authenticated gold discovery March 9, 1842. Lopez pulled a wild onion plant from the soil while he and a companion were resting under an oak tree in Placentia Canyon. He found gold particles clinging to the roots of the onion plant. A plaque exists at the corner of I-15 and Lyons Ave., Newhall.

No. 169: DRUM BARRACKS became the United States headquarters for Southern California, Arizona, and New Mexico. It was a garrison and base for supplies, and a landmark of the Civil War in California. A marker is at 1053 Cary St., Wilmington.

No. 170: HANCOCK PARK LA BREA. The bones of thousands of prehistoric animals have been entrapped during the Ice Age in pools of tar. The site was presented to the County of Los Angeles by Captain G. Allan Hancock. A marker is 5801 Wilshire Blvd., Los Angeles.

No. 171: MERCED THEATRE. It was built on North Main St. in 1870 next to the Pico House. It was built by William Abbot, a cabinet maker and named in honor of his wife, Merced Garcia. A marker is at 420 Main St., Los Angeles.

No. 172: PIONEER OIL REFINERY. The Star Oil Company, a predecessor of Standard Oil Company of California, drilled its first well in Pico Canyon. It yielded 100 barrels per day. The well resulted in the building of the first commercial oil refinery in California. A marker is at 238 Pine St., Newhall.

No. 235: CASA ADOBE DE SAN RAFAEL. In October, 1874 Jose Maria Verdugo petitioned Governor Pedro Fages for a grant of land. It was [the first and one of the largest made. When parts of Rancho San Rafael was sold, Tomas Sanchez, Sheriff of Los Angeles County, purchased a tract of 100 acres in 1865 and built an artistic adobe hacienda. A marker is located at 1330 Dorothy Dr., Glendale.

No. 289: FIRST HOME OF POMONA COLLEGE. Pomona College held its first classes in this small frame cottage on September 12. 1888. There was a mere handful of students, five faculty members and the president, Professor Edwin C. Norton. In January 1889, the college moved to an unfinished boom hotel in the town of Claremont. A marker is at corner of Mission Blvd., and White St., Pomona.

No. 301: LUGO ADOBE was built in 1840 by Don Vicente Lugo, one of the very few successful twe-story houses in the pueblo of Los Angeles. In 1867, Lugo donated the house on the plaza to St. Vincent's School (Forerunner of Loyola University) A marker is at Los Angeles and Alameda Streets, Los Angeles.

No. 302: THE OLD MILL, El Molino Viejo, was designed by Father Jose Maria Zalvidea and built of fired bricks and adobe in 1816. The mill was to serve Mission San Gabriel. Another grist mill was built in 1823 near the mission. Henry E. Huntington bought the building and used it for a golf clubhouse. The mill was restored in 1928. A marker is at 1120 Old Mill Road, San Marino.

No. 362: ROMULO PICO ADOBE (Ranchito Romulo) The oldest portion of the adobe was built in 1834 by ex-mission Indians. An upper story was added in 1874. A marker is at 10940 N Sepulveda Blvd., Mission Hills.

No. 363: CENTINELA SPRINGS. Bubbling springs once flowed here from their source in a deep water basin. The basin has existed continuously since the Pleistocene Era. Prehistoric animals, Indians, and early Inglewood settlers were attracted here by the artesian water. The springs were named after sentinels guarding cattle in the area. The springs and a marker are located in Centinela Park, 700 Warren Lane, Inglewood.

No, 367: E.J. BALDWIN'S QUEEN ANNE COTTAGE. It was designed by A.A. Bennett for entertaining. It was constructed by Elias (Lucky) Baldwin in 1881. Since there was no kitchen, meals were served from the nearby adobe where Baldwin actually lived. It is now part of the Los Angeles County Arboretum where a marker is located at 301 N. Baldwin, Arcadia.

NO. 368: REID-BALDWIN ADOBE. Hugo Reid, a Scotsman, petitioned the government of Mexico to grant him Rancho Santa Anita. His claim was strengthened by his marriage to Victoria, a native Indian of the San Gabriel Mission. He received the grant on April 16, 1841. He immediately started farming the property and planting vineyards. He built the Hugo Reid Adobe in 1839. E.J. Baldwin purchased the rancho in 1879 and added a wooden wing to the old adobe. See the marker at 301 N. Baldwin Ave., Arcadia.

No. 372: ADOBE DE PALOMARES. It was completed in 1854 and restored in 1939. It was the family home of Don Ygnacio Palomares. Governor Juan B. Alvarado granted Rancho San Jose to Don Ygnacio and Don Ricardo Vejar in 1837. See the marker at 491 E. Arrowhead Highway, Pomona.

No. 373: OLD SALT LAKE. Indians obtained salt from this lake. Sometime in the 1850s, Johnson and Allanson erected the necessary equipment to manufacture salt. See the marker at Harbor Dr. and Yacht Club Way, Redondo Beach.

No. 380: HOME OF DIEGO SEPULVEDA. This adobe home was built in the 1850s. It was the first two-story Monterey-type adobe built in Southern California. The home and a marker are in the 700 block of Channel St., San Pedro.

No. 381: OLD WHALING STATION. The whaling industry was started by a Captain Clark in 1864. It was abandoned in 1877. A marker is at the Portuguese Men's Club, Rancho Palos Verdes.

No. 383: ADOBE HOME OF JOSE DELORES SEPULVEDA. The adobe was built in 1818, but Sepulveda had trouble getting the land cleared. He went to Monterey to get the matter settled. On his return trip he was shot with an arrow by a hostile Indian. A marker is at Madison St. and Courtney Way, Torrance.

No. 384: TIMMS' POINT AND LANDING. In 1852 German emigrant Augustus W. Timms obtained Sepulveda's Landing on the mudflats near San Pedro. A marker is at Sampson Way at Southern Pacific Slip, San Pedro.

No. 385: RIO SAN GABRIEL BATTLEFIELD. American forces commanded by Robert F. Stockton, U.S. Navy Commander and Chief, and Brigadier General Stephan W. Kearney, U.S. Army, fought Californians commanded by General Jose Maria Flores. The battle was called the "*Battle of the Rio San Gabriel*". A marker is at Washington and Bluff Road, Montebello.

No. 386: LA CASA DE CARRION was built in 1886 by Saturnino Carrion and restored in 1951. A marker is located at 919 Puddingstone Dr., La Verne.

No. 387: ORTEGA-VIGARE ADOBE. It was built during the mission days of 1792-1805. It is the second oldest house in the region. A marker is at 616 Ramona St. San Gabriel.

No. 514: POMONA WATER POWER PLANT. It was the first hydroelectric installation in California for long-distance transmission of alternating current at high voltage. It was built in 1892 on San Antonio Creek. The first high voltage transformers provided 10,000 volts from the plant to Pomona.

No. 516: WELL, CSO 4 (PICO 4) It was the first commercially productive well. It was spudded in 1876 by Demetrius G. Schofield who became the first president of Standard Oil Company. At a depth of 300 feet, the well produced 30 barrels per day. When it was deepened to 600 feet, it produced 150 barrels per day. A marker Is located in Newhall.

No. 516-2: MENTRYVILLE is named after Charles Alexander Mentry, who in 11876 drilled the first successful oil well in California. His Star Oil Company was one of the predecessors of Standard Oil of California. See the marker at 27201 W. Pico Canyon Rd., Newhall.

No. 522: SERRA SPRINGS. The Portola Expedition camped at this spring. It's said that in 1770 Father Junipero said Mass here. The spring was once the water supply for the town of Santa Monica. It and a marker are located at 11800 Texas Ave. Los Angeles.

No. 531: LUMMIS HOME. This building was constructed by Charles F. Lummis in (1859-1928). Lummis was an author, editor, poet, athlete, librarian, historian, archeologist among other skills. A marker is located at 200 E Ave 43, Los Angeles.

No. 536: ORIGINAL BUILDING OF THE UNIVERSITY OF CALIFORNIA has been in continuous for educational purposes since October 6, 1880.

No. 554: CECIL B. DEMILLE BARN: Demille rented half of the barn as the studio where he made his first feature-length movie. It was called "The Squaw" man and was made in 1913. In 1927, the barn was transferred to Paramount Studios. A marker is at 2100 N. Highland Ave., Hollywood.

No. 556: RANCHO SAN FRANCISCO. The adobe building was built in 1804 as a granary Mission Sam Fernando. The rancho was granted to Antonio de Valle in 1839. William Lewis Manley and John Rogers obtained supplies and animals to rescue their comrades in a California-bound emigrant party stranded and starving in Death Valley. See the marker at corner of The Old Road and Henry Mayo Dr.

No. 567: VINCENT'S PLACE. This was the site of Saint Vincent's College from 1868 to 1887. The college, now Loyola University, was founded by Vincentian Fathers in 1865. It was the first institution of higher learning in Southern California. A marker is at St. Vicente's Court, Los Angeles.

No. 580: WELL, ALAMITOS 1. One of the most famous wells, it started on March 23, 1921. It flowed 590 barrels a day when it was completed. A marker is at Temple Ave and Hill St., Signal Hill.

No. 590: LANG. Charles Crocker on September 5, 1876, drove a golden spike here to complete his company's San Joaquin Valley line. A marker is Soledad Canyon.

No. 632: OLD SHORT CUT is California's first ranger station. It was built in 1900 by Louie Newcomb and Phillip Begue. The cabin took its name from the "Shortcut Canyon Trail ". A marker can be found at Angeles National Forest, Chilao Visitor's Center.

No. 637: CATALINA ADOBE. San Rafael was granted to Jose Maria Verdugo October 20, 1784. Don Jose died in 1831, leaving his estate to his son Julio and his blind daughter, Catalina. This adobe was built for Dona Catalina in the 1830s. She lived there until her death in the 1830s. It's located at 2211 Bonita Dr., Glendale.

No 646: GRAVE OF GEORGE CARALAMO (Greek George). Greek George was a camel driver who came to the United States with the second load of camels purchased by the War Department. A marker is located at Founder's Memorial Park, Whittier.

No. 653: THE CASCADES. This is a terminus for the Los Angeles-Owens River water. The great Aqueduct was completed in 1913. A marker is Foothill and Balboa Blvd., San Fernando.

No. 655: PORTOLA TRAIL CAMPSITE (1). Spanish colonization of California began in 1769 with the expedition of Don Gaspar de Portola from Mexico. A marker is Broadway and Elysian Park, Los Angeles.

No. 656: BELLA UNION HOTEL was a social and political center. The first Butterfield stagecoach from the east stopped here 21 days after leaving St. Louis. A marker is located at Fletcher Bowron Square, Los Angeles.

No. 658: WESTERN HOTEL. It was built by the Gilroy family in 1876. The Lancaster Chamber of Commerce was organized in its dining room. Amarker is located at 557 W. Lancaster Blvd., Lancaster.

No. 664: HERITAGE HOUSE. The house had only two rooms when it was built in 1869. Other rooms were added by sequent occupants. It was marked as the oldest house in Compton in 1955. It and a marker sit at Willowbrook and Myrrh St., Compton.

No. 665: PORTOLA TRAIL CAMPSITE, 2. The expedition of Don Gaspar de Portola from Mexico stopped here with his men. A marker is at 325 South La Cienega, Beverly Hills.

No. 669: GOVERNOR STONEMAN ADOBE. This was the site of “Los Robles”, the 400-acre estate of Governor George Stoneman. President Rutherford B. Hayes was entertained there in 1880. A marker is at 1912 Montrobles Place, San Marino.

No. 681: PARADOX HYBRID WALNUT TREE. It was planted in 1907 by George Weinshank as part of an experiment for the University of California. A marker located at 12300 Whittier Boulevard, Venice.

No. 688: LYONS STATION STAGE STOP. This was a combination store, post office, telegraph office, tavern and stage depot. You'll find the marker at 23287 N. Sierra Highway, Newhall.

No. 689: LOS ENCINOS STATE HISTORIC PARK. The Franciscan padres used Encino as their headquarters while exploring the valley before establishing Mission San Fernando in 1797. A marker is located at Los Encinos State Park, Encino.

No. 716: GRIFFITH RANCH. It was part of the San Fernando Mission lands. It was purchased by David Wark Griffith, pioneer of silent motion pictures. A marker is 12685 Foothill Blvd., San Fernando.

No. 717: THE ANGELES NATIONAL FOREST. It was the first national forest in California and the second in the United States. It was created by President Benjamin Harrison in 1892. It was first called "San Gabriel Timberland Reserve".

No. 718: SITE OF THE INITIAL U.S. AIR MEET. On Dominguez Hill in historic Rancho San Pedro, the first air meet in the U.S. was held January 10-20, 1910. A marker is located at 18501 S. Wilmington Ave., Carson.

No. 730: OLD PLAZA FIREHOUSE. It was dedicated to the firemen of Los Angeles Fire Department for their courage and faithful devotion to duty. This was the first building constructed as a fire station in Los Angeles. It's at 501 N. Los Angeles St.

No. 744: THE MIRROR BUILDING. The Butterfield Overland Mail Company took an option on this property in 1858 and acquired it in 1859. The large brick building contained offices and living quarters. A marker is at 145 S. Spring St., Los Angeles.

No. 753: SAN FERNANDO CEMETERY. It was earlier known as the Morningside Cemetery. It is the oldest non-sectarian cemetery in the San Fernando Valley. A marker is at SW corner of Bledsoe and Foothill in Sylmar.

No. 789: SITE OF THE LOS ANGELES STAR. This was Southern California's first newspaper. It suspended operation temporarily from 1864 to 1868. A marker is located at 145 Spring St., Los Angeles.

No. 822: FIRST JEWISH SITE IN LOS ANGELES. The Hebrew Benevolent Society of Los Angeles was the first benevolent organization in the city. A marker is located at 800 W. Lilac Terrace, Los Angeles.

No. 840: OLD SANTA MONICA FORESTRY STATION. In 1877, the State Board of Forestry established the nation's first experiment station. Marker is at corner of Latimer and Hilltree Rds., Los Angeles.

No. 871: THE GAMBLE HOUSE. It was built in 1908 and is considered a tribute to the genius of architects Charles Sumner Greene and Henry Mather Greene. A marker is at 4 Westmoreland Place, Pasadena.

No. 874: WORKMAN HOME and family cemetery. William Workman and John Rowland organized the first wagon train of permanent settlers. The train arrived in Southern California in 1841. Together Workman and Rowland owned and developed the 48,790-acre La Puente Rancho. It's located at 15415 E. Don Julian Rd., City of Industry.

No. 881: PORT OF LOS ANGELES LONG WHARF. In 1893 the Southern Pacific Railroad Company completed its 4,720-foot wharf. A marker is at Will Rogers State Beach, Pacific Palisades.

No. 887: PASADENA PLAYHOUSE. It was founded in 1917 by Gilmor Brown. The Pasadena Playhouse was designed by architect Elmer Grey. It was given the honorary title,"State Theatre of California" by the California Legislature. It's at 39 El Molino Ave., Pasadena.

No. 894: S.S. CATALINA. It was commonly referred to as the Great White Steamer. The ship was specially built by William Wrigley to serve his Catalina Island as a passenger ferry. During World War II she was requisitioned for use as a troop carrier. In 1946, she resumed her voyages to Avalon. A marker is the Port Of Los Angeles. Berth 36.

No. 894: CHATSWORTH CALERA SITE This is one of the few surviving structures of the early 19th century lime industry.. A marker is on State Highway 27 and Plummer., Chatsworth.

No. 919: ST. FRANCIS DAM DISASTER SITE. The 185-foot concrete St. Francis Dam was part of the Los Angeles aqueduct system. On March 12, 1928, just before midnight, the dam collapsed and sent more than twelve billion gallons of water roaring down the valley of the Santa Clara River. More than 450 lives were lost. It's located in Saugus.

No. 920: Casa de San Pedro. It's the first known commercial structure on the shore of San Pedro Bay. It was built in 1823 by the trading firm of McCulloch and Hartnell to store cattle hides from the San Gabriel and San Fernando missions. Richard Henry Dana described this building in his novel, "Two Years Before the Mast". A marker is in the 2400 block of Pacific Ave., San Pedro.

No. 933: SITE OF LLANO DEL RIO cooperative colony. This was a non-religious Utopian experiment. Its founder Job Harriman, was an influential socialist leader. At its height, the colony contained a thousand members. A marker is located on State Highway 138, Llano.

No. 934: DETENTION CAMPS FOR JAPANESE. Detention camps were located at both Santa Anita and at Pomona. There was a mass incarceration of 97,785 Californians of Japanese ancestry during World War II. Detention camps were located at both Arcadia and at Pomona. A marker is at Ardadia and Pomona.

No. 939: TWENTIETH CENTURY FOLK ART OLD TRAPPERS LODGE: Old Trapper's Lodge is one of California's 20th Century Folk Art Experiments. It represents the life work of John Ehn, a self-taught artist who wished to pass on a sense of the Old West. A marker isnow at 6201 Winnetka Ave., Woodland Hills.

No. 947: REFORM SCHOOL FOR JUVENILE OFFENDERS (FRED C. NELLES SCHOOL) On March 11, 1889, the California Legislature authorized the establishment of a school for juvenile offenders. The Whittier State School for boys and girls opened on July 1, 1891. Girls were transferred in 1916 and only boys have been in residence since that time. A marker is located at 11850 East Whittier Blvd., Whittier.

No. 960: LOSE ANGELES MEMORIAL COLISEUM. This stadium was completed in 1923. It is the first stadium to host the Olympic Games twice. A marker is at 3911 S. Figueroa, Los Angeles.

No. 961: HAROLD LLOYD ESTATE (GREENACRES) Green Acres is one of the great estates of Hollywood's Golden Era. It was built in 1929 for Harold Lloyd, the silent screen comedian. It is of Mediterranean/Italian Renaissance style. It contains 44 rooms. See the marker at 1740 Green Acres Place, Beverly Hills.

No. 963: THE MOJAVE ROAD. Long ago, Mojave Indians used a network of pathways to cross the Mojave Desert. In 1826, American trapper Jedediah Smith used their paths and became the first non-Indian to reach the California coast overland from mid-America. A marker is at Drum Barracks, Los Angeles.

No, 965: POINT DUME. In 1793, English explorer George Vancouver commanded an expedition to determine the extent of settlement of the northwest coast of America. He named this rocky promontory Point Dume after his Franciscan friend, Father Francisco Dumetz. A marker is at Point Dume State Beach, Malibu.

No. 966: ADAMSON HOUSE AT MALIBU LAGOON STATE BEACH. Designed by Stiles O. Clements in 1929, this Spanish Colonial Revival home contains the best examples of decorative ceramic tile produced by Malibu Potteries. A marker is at 23200 Pacific Coast Highway, Malibu.

No. 972: NAVY AND MARINE CORPS RESERVE CENTER. Designed as the largest enclosed structure without walls in the world, California architects Robert Clements and Associates, this structure was built by WPA in 1938. See the marker at 1700 Stadium Way, Los Angeles.

No. 975: EL MONTE-FIRST SOUTHERN SETTLEMENT BY EMIGRANTS FROM UNITED STATES. El Monte played a significant part in California's Pioneer History. It was first an encampment on the Old Spanish Trail. By the 1850s, some began to call El Monte the "End of the Old Spanish Trail". A plaque is located in the Santa Fe Trail Historical Park, El Monte.

No. 978: RANCHO LOS CERRITOS HISTORIC SITE: This 27,000-acre rancho was once part of an 18th century Spanish land grant to soldier Manuel Nieto. He built a Monterey-style adobe in 1844. It served the Temple and Bixby families as headquarters for their large-scale cattle and sheep ranching operation. In the 1880s, the land was subdivide for farming and city development. Its marker is located at 4600 Virginia Road, Long Beach.

No. 984: CASA DE RANCHO SAN ANTONIO (Henry Gage Mansion) Here in this house is the remaining portions of an adobe built by Francisco Salvador Lugo and his son, Antonio Maria Lugo. Francisco Lugo was a prominent early landholder and Antonio served as Alcalde of Los Angeles. Henry Tift Gage acquired the property in 1880 and lived there from 1883 until 1924. Gage served as Governor of California from 1899 to 1903. The mansion and marker are located at 7000 E. Gage, Bell Gardens.

No. 988: PACIFIC ASIA MUSEUM. Grace Nicholson was a collector and authority on American Indian and Asian Art and artifacts. Her museum has been called an outstanding example of 1920s revival architecture and is unique for its use of Chinese ornamentation. See the marker at 46 North Los Robles Ave., Pasadena.

No. 990: CHRISTMAS TREE LANE. The 135 Deodar Cedar trees were planted in 1885 by the Woodbury family. In 1920, F.C. Nash organized the "Mile of Christmas Trees". The trees have been strung with 10,000 lights each holiday season. They are located on Santa Rosa Ave. from Woodbury Ave. to Altadena Dr., Pasadena.

No. 993: WATTS TOWERS OF SIMON RODIA. Watts Towers are perhaps the nation's best-known work of folk art sculpture. Using simple hand tools, cast-off materials (glass, shell, pottery pieces, and broken tile), Italian immigrant Simon Rodia spent 30 years building a tribute to his adopted country. It's at 1765 East 107th St., Los Angeles.

No. 997: TUNA CLUB OF AVALON. The Tuna Club of Avalon marks the birthplace of modern big game sportfishing in 1898. Led by Dr. Charles Frederick Holder, the club's founding members adopted rules of conduct stressing conservationist ethics and sporting behavior. Its marker is located at 100 St. Catherine Way, Avalon.

No. 1006: BEALES CUT STAGECOACH PASS. Beale's Cut is the only physical and cultural feature of its kind in the entire Los Angeles Basin. The creation and maintenance of the cut across the San Gabriel and Santa Susana Mountain ranges made mountains passable. A marker is located at Sierra Highway and Clampitt Road, Santa Clarita.

No. 1011: FRANK LLOYD WRIGHT TEXTILE BLOCK HOUSES (Ennis House). The Ennis House was designed by Frank Lloyd Wright and built in 1924 for Charles and Mabel Ennis. It's located at 2655 Glendower Ave., Los Angeles.

No. 1011: FRANK LLOYD WRIGHT TEXTILE BLOCK HOUSE (Freeman House) The Samuel and Harriet Freeman House was built in 1924. It is one of four residences designed by Frank Lloyd Wright that was designed to be affordable using cheap building material if concrete. Find the marker at 1962 Glencoe Way, Los Angeles.

No. 1014: LONG BEACH MARINE STADIUM. It was created in 1932 for rowing events of the Xth Olympiad. The stadium was the first man-made rowing course in the United States. A marker is at Pete /archer Rowing Center, Long Beach.

No. 1018: MANHATTAN BEACH STATE PIER. This pier was constructed during the years 1917-1920. The roundhouse building was added a year later. The rounded end of the pier helped to withstand the pounding of the Pacific. A marker is in Manhattan Beach.

No. 1021: LIBERTY HILL SITE. In 1923, the Marine Transport Workers Industrial Union 510 called a strike that immobilized 90 ships in San Pedro. The union protested low wages, bad working conditions and the imprisonment of union activists. Denied access to public property, strikers rallied at the site now called "Liberty Hill". A marker is at 5th and Harbor, San Pedro.

No. 1038: HAY TREE. The tree is a rare remnant of the city's once-thriving dairy and hay industry. There are no other properties in Paramount linked to the hay industry except for this tree. It's at 16475 Paramount Blvd., Paramount.

No. 1041: SITE OF THE CHILDHOOD HOME OF THE BEACH BOYS. It was here that Brian, Dennis and Carl Wilson developed their unique musical skills. It was here in 1961 that they, their cousin Mike Love, and friend Al Jardine, gathered to record their breakthrough song "Surfin". It's located at W. 119th Street, Hawthorne.

Madera County

No. 1001: CALIFORNIA NATIVE AMERICAN CEREMONIAL ROUNDHOUSES (WASSAMA ROUNDHOUSE). The Wassama Roundhouse dates to the 1860s. It was reconstructed in 1985 on the same location as the previous four houses. It served as the focal point of spiritual and ceremonial ife for many Native Californians. Take Highway 49 to Ahwahnee and then east four miles on Round House Road.

Marin County

No. 207: FIRST SAWMILL IN MARIN COUNTY. This mill was built by John Reed about 1833-34 on Rancho Corte Madera del Presidio. It was considered the wood-cutting place for Mill Valley. Reed built the first house in Sausalito and the first ferryboat to ply San Francisco Bay. A marker is at Blithedale and Tower, Dr.

No. 210: OLDEST HOUSE NORTH OF SAN FRANCISCO BAY. This house was built in 1776 by the father of Camillo Ynitia or Unitia, the last chief of the Olompali Indians. The Indians were taught to make adobe bricks by Lieutenant Bodega and his party while they were surveying and charting the harbor of San Francisco Bay. A marker is located at Olompali State Historic Park, 8901 Redwood Highway on State Highway 101.

No. 220: MISSION SAN RAFAEL ARCANGEL The San Rafael Arcángel Mission is the 20th in the chain of the 21 California missions. A marker is at 5th and A Street, San Rafael.

No. 221: SITE OF THE LIGHTER WHARF AT BOLINAS. The wharf was built in the 1850s to load lumber to be floated on lighters out to the deeper water near the channel, where it was transferred to seagoing vessels for shipment to San Francisco. A marker is at the end of Bolinas Lagoon, Bolinas.

No. 222: LIME KILNS. Tradition is that the lime kilns were built by Russian stone masons and worked by Indians during the Russian occupation of Sonoma County. The Russians used the lime to whitewash their windmills, farm buildings, granaries, storehouses, and cattle yards, to tan hides, and to manufacture brick and tile. A marker is 4.5 miles south of Olema.

No. 529: ANGEL ISLAND. In 1775, the packet San Carlos, was the first known ship to enter San Francisco Bay. It anchored in this cove at Angel Island. A marker is located at Hospital Cove, Angel Island Park.

No. 552: PIONEER PAPER MILL. The first paper mill on the Pacific Coast was built here in November 1856 by Samuel Penfield Taylor. It first used water power and then later steam to power the mill. The mill was closed by the depression of 1893. It was destroyed by fire in 1915. Its marker is inside Samuel P. Taylor State Park, Lagunitas.

No. 630: ST. VINCENT'S SCHOOL FOR BOYS. In 1853, Timothy Murphy gave 317-acres of land to Archbishop Alemany for educational purposes. Here, in 1855, the Sisters of Charity founded St. Vincent's school for boys. A marker is on Highway 101 on St. Vincent Dr., San Rafael.

No. 679: HOME OF LORD CHARLES SNOWDEN FAIRFAX. Charles Fairfax was an assemblyman, Speaker of the Assembly, and Clerk of the State Supreme Court. A descendent of Scottish barons of the Cameron Fairfax family of Virginia, Fairfax was involved in the last of California's historic political duels as host to the principals and friend of two antagonists. It's located at Pastori and Belmont Ave., Fairfax.

No. 917: GREEN BRAE BRICK KILN: This brick kiln on San Quentin Peninsula is the only surviving structure of the Remillard Brick Company. It provided brick for use in Ghiradelli Square, the Palace Hotel, and other San Francisco structures after the 1906 earthquake. A marker is at Marin Town and Country Club.

No. 922: OUTDOOR ART CLUB. The Outdoor Art Club was designed by Bernard Maybeck in 1904. It is particularly notable for its unusual roof truss system. It was founded in 1902 by 35 Mill Valley women. It's located one mile west of Blithedale Ave. at Throckmorton, Mill Valley.

No. 924: CHINA CAMP. This was one of the earliest, largest and most productive fishing villages in California. The Chinese introduced the use of commercial netting to catch bay shrimp off Point San Pedro. China Camp is the last surviving Chinese shrimp fishing village in California. It's located at Santa Venetia.

No. 974: GOLDEN GATE BRIDGE. Construction began in 1933 on the Golden Gate Bridge. Engineer Joseph Strauss and Arcitect Irving Morrow created the extraordinarily beautiful bridge. The designs for the Golden Gate Bridge show the greatest attention to detail, especially on the two streamlined modern towers. The bridge's 4,200 feet of clear span from tower to tower was the longest in the world until 1959. A marker is located in the observation area.

No. 999: MARIN COUNTY CIVIC CENTER. This Civic Center Complex was designed by Frank Lloyd Wright near the end of his long career. They are the only government buildings designed by the famous architect that were ever constructed. The structures were designed to "melt into the sunburnt hills". A marker is at Civic Center, San Rafael.

Mariposa County

No. 323: MORMON BAR. Mormon Bar was first mined in 1849 by members of the Mormon Battalion. They stayed only a short time and their places were taken at once by other miners. Later, thousands of Chinese worked the same ground again. It's 1.8 miles south of Mariposa.

No. 331: BEAR VALLEY. It was first called Johnsonville. Bear Valley had a population of 3,000, including Chinese, Cornish and Mexicans. Still standing are Bon Ton Saloon, Trabucco Store, Odd Fellows Hall, a school house and he remains of a jail. A marker is on Highway 49, Bear Valley.

No. 332: COULTERVILLE. George W. Coulter started a tent store here in 1850 to supply he hundreds of miners working the rich placers of Maxwell, Boneyard, and Black Creeks. He built the first hotel. Water for it was pumped by two Newfoundland dogs. A marker is in County Park, Coulterville.

No. 333: HORNITOS. Hornitos means "little ovens" in Spanish and derives its name from the many old Mexican graves in the shape oof little square bake ovens set on top of the ground. The town was settled by an undesirable element driven out of the adjoining town of Quartzburg. A marker is on Bear Valley Road, Hornitos.

No. 518: AGUA FRIA. This was the first county seat of Mariposa County, one of the original 27 counties in California. At that time, Mariposa County comprised one-sixth of the state. It became the seat of government in 1852. Agua Fria and its marker is located 3.2 miles West of Mariposa.

No. 527: SAVAGE TRADING POST. It was here that James D. Savage established a store built of logs in 1849. In the spring of 1850, fearing Indian depredations, he moved to Mariposa Creek. In December, his store was pillaged and burned. A marker is on Highway 140.

No. 670: MARIPOSA COUNTY COURTHOUSE. This is the oldest court of law in California and has served continuously as the seat of government since 1854. Much of U.S. mining law is based on decisions emanating from this historic courthouse. It's at 10th and Bullion Sts., Mariposa.

No. 790: YOSEMITE VALLEY. President Abraham Lincoln, on June 30, 1864, signed an act granting the Yosemite Valley and the Mariposa Big Tree Grove to the State of California. The properties were to be used for public use, resort and recreation. This was the first federal authorization to preserve scenic and scientific values for public benefit. A plaque is mounted on entrance to auditorium building, Visitor Center.

Mendocino County

No. 549: FROG WOMAN ROCK. This site is associated with the Pomo legend of Frog Woman, the clever and powerful wife of Coyote, who lived near this rock. It's located six miles south of Hopland on Highway 101.

No. 615: FORT BRAGG. The Fort was established June 11, 1857 by 1st Lieutenant Horatio Gates Gibson, 3rd Artillery, U.S. Army. He named it in honor of his former company commander, Braxton Bragg. The fort was abandoned in 1864. It's at 321 Main St., Fort Bragg.

No. 674: ROUND VALLEY. The valley was discovered by Frank M. Azbill, who arrived from Eden Valley May 15, 1854. Charles Kelsey from Clear Lake and George E. White visited it. It's on State Highway 162 five miles south of Covelo.

No. 714: MENDOCINO PREBYTERIAN CHURCH. This is one of the oldest Protestant churches in continuous use in California. It was organized in 1859. A marker is at 44831 Main St., Mendocino.

No. 926: SUN HOUSE. Constructed in 1911, this house is a unique Craftsman style redwood building which incorporates northwestern designs into its architecture. It was designed by George Wilcox and John W. and Grace Carpenter Hudson. Dr. Hudson was a recognized authority on American Indians and Mrs. Hudson was an outstanding artist. A marker is at 431 South Main St., Ukiah.

No. 927: TEMPLE OF KWAN TAI. It is one of the oldest of California's Chinese houses of worship in continuous use. The temple may date back as far as 1854. The Chinese built many temples in California, but most have been destroyed and no others remain on the North Coast. It's located at 45160 Albion St., Mendocino.

No. 980: UKIAH VICHY SPRINGS RESORT. Frank Marble discovered these springs in 1848 and William Day established a resort here in the 1850s. It is one of the oldest and one of the few continuously operated mineral springs in California. It is the only mineral springs in California that resembles the famed Grand Grille Springs of Vichy, France. It's at 2701 Vichy Springs Road, Ukiah.

No. 1035: POINT ARENA LIGHT STATION. In 1889, the Point Arena Light Station was listed for its significance in the area of maritime history. Heavy storms along the coast made travel treacherous. It was constructed in 1870. It's at Lighthouse Road, Point Arena.

Merced County

No. 409: SNELLING COURTHOUSE. It is the first courthouse in Merced County. It was built in 1857. The historic monument was placed by the Native Sons of the Golden West on May 20, 1930. A marker is on Main St., Snelling.

No. 548: CANAL FARM INN. It's the original San Joaquin Valley ranch headquarters of cattle baron Henry Miller. Miller's farsighted planning and development in the 1870s of a vast gravity irrigation system and the founding of Los Banos in 1889, provided the basis for the area's present wealth and stability. It's at 1460 East Pacheco Blvd., Los Banos.

No. 550: LOS BANOS. Los Banos (the baths) Del Padre Arroyo was visited in 1805 by Spanish explorers. Its name was changed to Los Banos Creek by American emigrants. A marker is at 803 E. Pacheco Blvd, Los Banos.

No. 829: PACHECO PASS. Lieutenant made his first exploratory journey into the San Joaquin Valley in 1805. Since then, it has been trail, toll road, stagecoach road, and freeway. It's the principal route between the coastal areas to the west and the great valley and mountains to the east. A marker is at the Romero Overlook, San Luis Reservoir.

No. 934: TEMPORARY DETENTION CAMPS FOR JAPANESE-AMERICANS-MERCED ASSEMBLY CENTER. This was one of 15 temporary detention camps established during World War II to incarcerate persons of Japanese ancestry, a majority who were American citizens. A marker is located at the Merced County Fairgrounds.

Modoc County

No. 6: FREMONT'S CAMP. John C. Fremont's expedition from Fort Sutter to Upper Klamath Lake camped here in 1846. They were the first non-Indians to pass this way. A marker is on Alturas Highway, Tule Lake.

No. 8: BLOODY POINT. In 1850, one of the bloodiest massacres of emigrants ever known occurred here when Modoc Indians killed more than 90 men, women and children in a surprise attack. A year later, another large party narrowly escaped the same fate. It's located 8.3 miles Northwest of State Highway 139, East of Tule Lake.

No. 14: CRESSLER AND BONNER TRADING POST. Cressler and Bonner started the first mercantile establishment in Modoc County at this location. It was the first building erected in the town of Cedarville. It's located in Cedarville Park between Bonner and Townsend Sts., Cedarville.

No. 15: BONNER GRADE. The first road from Cedarville to Alturas followed the course of the present highway over the Warner Mountains from Surprise Valley. A marker is located on State Highway 299, 6.2 miles West of Cedarville.

No. 16: INFERNAL CAVERNS BATTLEGROUND, 1857. A battle between U.S. troops and Shoshone, Paiute and Pit Indians occurred here in 1867. The Indians took refuge in a series of caverns located at the top of a rocky slope. A marker is on Ferry Ranch Road, Likely.

No. 108: BATTLE OF LAND'S RANCH. One of the engagements of the Modoc War took place here on December 21, 1872 on what is known as Land's Ranch. Two men were killed and several were wounded. It was at State Highway 139 and County Road 114, Tule Lake.

No. 109: CHIMNEY ROCK: The chimney was cut out of solid rock by Thomas L. Denson, who came west by the Santa Fe Trail in 1870. Denson built his cabin alongside a pyramid shaped rock, cutting the fireplace and flue out of the solid rock itself. A marker is beside the railroad on State Highway 395.

No. 111: OLD EMIGRANT TRAIL. This old pioneer trail is part of one of the earliest roads in Northeastern California. Trees eight to 10-inches in diameter are growing in the old road bed. Its marker is 9.3 miles Northwest of Canby.

No. 125: EVANS AND BAILEY FIGHT-1861. S.D. Evans, Sr. and Joe Bailey, were stockmen from Rogue River Valley, Oregon. They and 16 of their employees were driving 900 head of cattle from Roseburg to the mines at Virginia City when they were attacked by Indians. The two owners were killed. A marker is located on top of a hill, 500 feet South of Centerville Rd., Canby.

No. 430: FORT BIDWELL. It's named for John Bidwell and was established in 1865. The fort operated until 1893. From 1898 to 1930, the fort served as a non-reservation boarding school for Indians. A marker is at the west end of Bridge St., Fort Bidwell.

No. 546: APPLEGATE-LASSEN EMIGRANT TRAIL (FANDANGO PASS. This spot marks the convergence of two trails used by emigrants during the years 1846-1850. The Applegate Trail led from the Humboldt River in Nevada to the Willamette Valley in Oregon. The Lassen Cutoff turned south at Goose Lake to the northern mines in California. A marker is at Fandango Pass.

No. 850-2: TULE LAKE RELOCATION CENTER. Tule Lake was one of the American concentration camps established during World War II to incarcerate 110,000 persons of Japanese ancestry. A marker is at State Highway 139 and County Road 176.

Mono County

No. 341: BODIE. Gold was discovered here in 1859 by William S. Bodey after whom the town was named. Bodie's mines produced gold valued at more than 100 million dollars. Bodie is one of the best known California ghost towns. A marker is in Bodie State Park.

No. 792: DOG TOWN. The first major gold rush on the eastern slope of the Sierra Nevada, Dog Town derived its name from a popular miners' term for camps with huts or hovels. Ruins lying close to the cliff bordering Dog Town Creek are all that remains of the makeshift dwellings which formed part of the 'diggins' here. A marker may be in place on State Highway 395, Bridgeport.

No. 995-1: TRAIL OF THE JOHN C. FREMENT 1884 EXPEDITION. In 1884, while mapping the western United States, Lt. John C. Fremont's party passed through northern Mono County. After passing through Mono County, Fremont passed over the Sierra to Sutter's Fort in the Sacramento Valley. A marker is at Big Bend-Mountain Gate, Bridgeport.

Monterey County

No. 1: CUSTOM HOUSE. Commodore John Drake Sloat raised the American flag over this building on July 7, 1846 to signal the passing of California from Mexican to American rule. Custom House was restored through the efforts of the Native Sons of the Golden West with the assistance of the people of California. It an its marker sit between Scott and Decatur Sts., Monterey.

No. 105: ROYAL PRESIDIO CHAPEL OF SAN CARLOS BORROMEO. It was established as a mission by Father Junipero Serra in 1770. This became the royal Presidio Chapel when the mission was moved to Carmel. It's located at 550 Church Street, Monterey.

No. 106: LARKIN HOUSE. The adobe-and-wood Larkin House was built in 1835 by Thomas Oliver Larkin. He was a Yankee merchant who came to California in 1832. Since he was the only U.S. consul to California under Mexican rule, his home became the American consulate from 1844 to 1846. It's at the corner of Jefferson and Calle Principal, Monterey.

No. 126: COLTON HALL. In this building met the convention that drafted the Constitution under which California was admitted to statehood on September 9, 1850. Rev. Walter Colton, first American Alcalde in Monterey, erected the building as a public hall and schoolhouse. It's between Jefferson and Madison, Monterey.

No. 128: LANDING PLACE FOR SEBASTIAN VIZCAINO AND FRAY JUNIPERO SERRA. Sebastian Vizcaino landed here December 17, 1602. Mass was sung by three Carmelite friars and the country was taken in the name of Spain. In the same spot, Fray Junipero Serra landed from the San Antonio on June 3, 1770 to join Captain Gaspar de Portola and Fray Juan Crespi. A marker is at Monterey State Park.

No. 136: FIRST THEATER IN CALIFORNIA. It was built in 1844 as a sailor's lodging by Jack Swan. In 1848, it was commandeered by a group of mustered-out soldiers of Colonel Stevenson's regiment of New Yorkers. It's on the corner of Scott and Pacific Streets, Monterey.

No. 232: MISSION SAN ANTONIO DE PADUA. The mission was established in 1771 and was the third in a series of missions founded by Father Junipero Serra. Its setting in the valley of the San Antonio River makes it one of the most outstanding examples of early mission life.

No. 233: MISSION NUESTRA SENORA DE LA SOLEDAD. This mission was founded in 1791 by Father Fermin Francisco de Lasuen. Governor Jose Joaquin de Arrillaga was buried there in 1814. The mission was prosperous in its early years but declined after 1825. Father Vicente Francisco Sarria stayed on in poverty to serve the Indians until his death in 1835. A marker is at Fort Romie Rd., Soledad.

No. 348: HOUSE OF GOVERNOR ALVARADO. A native of Monterey, Alvarado served as Governor of Mexican California from December 20, 1836 to December 20, 1842. During his administration, the increasing influx of Americans and the Russian settlement at Fort Ross began to be regarded as serious problems. It's located at 494-498 Alvarado St., Monterey.

No. 351: VASQUEZ HOUSE: This adobe house was occupied by a sister of Tiburcio Vasquez, the colorful bandit of the 1870s. It's at 546 Dutra St., Monterey.

No. 352: ROBERT LOUIS STEVENSON HOUSE. Essayist and storyteller Robert Louis Stevenson lived here in 1879. It's at 530 Houston St., Monterey.

No. 353: HOUSE OF FOUR WINDS. In the 1830s, Thomas Oliver Larkin built the House of Four Winds. It was named for the weather vane in his garden. You'll find a marker at 540 Calle Way, Monterey.

No. 354: OLD PACIFIC HOUSE. It was built as a hotel in 1835 by Jams McKinley. In later years it was law offices, a newspaper, small stores and a ballroom. In 1880 David Jack bought the property. Miss Margaret Jack made a gift of the property to the State of California. It's at Monterey State Historic Park, Custom House Plaza.

No. 387: THE GLASS HOUSE, CASA MATERNA OF THE VALLEJOS. In the 1920s, Don Ignacio Vallejo built the house on Bolsa de San Cayetano. Don Ignacio and Dona Maria Antonio Lugo y Vallejo had 13 children, one of whom was General Mariano Guadalupe Vallejo. It's located at Hillcrest and Salinas roads.

No. 494: RICHARDSON HOUSE. Los Coches Rancho (8,994-acres) was granted to Maria Josefa Soberanes de Richardson by the Mexican government in 1841. Her husband, William Bruner Richardson, built the house in 1843. The adobe was later used as a stage stop and post office. It was donated to the state of California by Margaret Jack in 1858. It's at the corner of State Highway 101 and Arroyo Seco Road.

No. 532: CASA DE ORO. In the 1850s this was a general merchandise store operated by Joseph Boston & Co. In later years it was called Casa de Oro because of the unverified story that it had been a gold depository. It's on the corner of Oliver and Scott, Monterey.

No. 560: HILL TOWN FERRY. It was operated by Hiram Cory. It was one of the first ferries across the Salinas River. The toll in 1877 was: buggy and horse, 25 cents; buggy and horses, 37 1/2 cents; four horses and wagon, 85 cents; six horses and wagon, $1; horse and saddle, 25 cents; and man on foot, 12 1/2 cents. The ferry operated until a bridge was built in 1889.

No. 651: BATTLE OF NATIVIDAD. American forces under Captains Charles D. Burrass and Bluford K. Thompson clashed with Comandante Manuel de Jesus Castro's Californios in 1846. The Americans saved a large herd of horses for Lt. Col. John C. Fremont who then proceeded south to participate in the Armistice at Cahuenga in 1847.

No. 712: SOBERANES ADOBE. Don Jose Estrada built this adobe in 1830. He sold the property to Don Feliciano Soberanes. The adobe was the home of the Soberanes family from 1860 to 1922, when Mr. and Mrs. William O'Donnell acquired it. Mrs. O'Donnell gave the property to the state in 1953. It's at 336 Pacific St., Monterey.

No. 713: GUTIERREZ ADOBE. In 1841, Monterey granted a lot to Joaquin Gutierrez where he and his wife built an adobe. The house has since been donated to the state.

No. 839: CHAUTAUQUA HALL. The first Chautauqua in the West was organized at Pacific Grove in 1879. It was designed to present moral attractions and the highest grade of concerts. It's at 16th and Central Ave. Pacific Grove.

No. 870: JOSE EUSEBIO BORONDA ADOBE CASA: It was built in 1844 and is an outstanding example of a Mexican-era rancho adobe. It's virtually unaltered since its construction. It's at 333 Boronda Rd. at W. Laurel Dr., Salinas.

No. 934: TEMPORARY DETENTION CAMPS FOR JAPANESE AMERICANS-SALINAS ASSEMBLY CENTER. From April to July, people of Japanese ancestry were confined in the Salinas Rodeo Grounds during World War II.

No. 951: LIGHT STATIONSS OF CALIFORNIA POINT SUR LIGHT STATION. Spanish explorers and later New England hide and tallow traders found the big Sur coastline a great hazard. Heavy fogs and extreme winds caused the wreck of many vessels on this coast. A lighthouse was clearly needed. Construction began in 1887 and the lamp was lit on August 1, 1889.

Napa County

No. 359: OLD BALE MILL. This historic gristmill was built by Dr. E.T. Bale, grantee of Carne Humana Rancho in 1846. The mill and the surrounding land was deeded to the Native Sons of the Golden West by Mrs. W.W. Lyman. It's located in Bale Memorial Park, Calistoga.

No. 547: CHILES MILL. Joseph Ballinger Chiles erected the mill on Rancho Catacula in 1845-56. It is the first American flour mill in Northern California. Chiles served as a vice president of the Society of California Pioneers, 1850-53. The mill is in St. Helena.

No. 561: SCHRAMSBERG. It was founded in 1862 by Jacob Shram. This was the first hillside winery in Napa Valley. Robert Louis Stevenson visited here in 1880. He devoted a chapter of his "Silverado Squatter" to Schramsburg and its wines. Ambrose Pierce and Lilly Hitchcock Coit were other cherished friends. It's at the end of Schramsburg road in Calistoga.

No. 563: CHARLES KRUG WINERY. It was founded in 1861 by Charles Krug. It is the oldest operating winery in Napa Valley. The pioneer winemaker made the first commercial wine in Napa County in 1858. Located at 2800 Main St., S. Helena.

No. 564: GEORGE YOUNT BLOCKHOUSE. This log block house was built in 1836 by George Calvert Yount. He was a pioneer settler in Napa County. Nearby was his adobe house, built in 1837. Across the bridge were his grist and saw mills, built in 1845. The property is located at Cook Rd. and Yount Mill Rd., Yountville.

No. 682: SITE OF YORK'S CABIN, CALISTOGA. Among the first houses in the area was John York's log cabin. It was built in 1845. It was razed in 1930. Calistoga was named by Sam Brannan. The site is located on Highway 29 and Lincoln Ave., Calistoga.

No. 683: SITE OF HUDSON CABIN, CALISTOGA. David Hudson was an early pioneer wjp purchased land, cleared it, and planted crops and built homes. Hudson built his cabin in 1845. It's at Wapoo Ave. and Grant St., Calistoga.

No. 684: SAM BRANNAN STORE, CALISTOGA. Sam Brannan arrived in the Napa Valley in the late 1850s. He purchased a square mile of land at the foot of Mount St. Helena. This is the store he built in which he made $50,000 in one year. It's at Wapoo Ave. and Grant St., Calistoga.

No. 685: SAM BRANNAN COTTAGE, CALISTOGA. Brannan dreamed of making Napa Valley the "Saratoga of California". In 1866, he built cottages and planted palm trees in preparation for the opening of the resort. It's at 1311 Washington St., Calistoga.

No. 686: SITE OF THE KELSEY HOUSE, CALISTOGA. Nancy Kelsey arrived in California in 1841 with the Bidwell-Bartleson party in 1841. She and her family settled down in Calistoga. Now the hearthstone is all that can be seen of the house. It's at State Highway 29 and Diamond Mountain Rd, Calistoga.

No. 687: NAPA VALLEY RAILROAD DEPOT, CALISTOGA. The railroad depot is now Southern Pacific depot. It was built in 1868. Its roundhouse across Lincoln Avenue is gone. On its first trip, this railroad brought people to Calistoga for the elaborate opening of Brannan's summer resort I n October, 1888. It's at 1458 Lincoln Ave. Calistoga.

No. 693: GRAVE OF GEORGE C. YOUNT. George C. Yount was the first United States citizen to be ceded a Spanish land grant in the Napa Valley. He was a skilled hunter, a frontiersman, a craftsman and a farmer. A friend to all, he was host of Caymus Rancho. He's buried in the Pioneer Cemetery, Lincoln and Jackson Sts., Yountville.

No. 710: ROBERT LOUIS STEVENSON STATE PARK. In the spring of 1880, Robert Louis Stevenson brought his bride to Silverado. He and Fannie Osbourne Stevenson lived here from May 19 until July while he gathered the notes for "Silverado Squatters".

No. 814: BERINGER BROTHERS WINERY. It was built by Frederick and Jacob Beringer. The winery has the distinction of never having ceased operating since its founding in 1876. The Beringers, in the European tradition, dug underground wine tunnels hundreds of feet in length. These tunnels maintain a constant temperature of 58 degrees. It's at 2000 Main St., St. Helena.

No. 828: VETERANS HOME OF CALIFORNIA. This home for California's aged and disabled veterans was established in 1884 by Mexican War veterans and members of the Grand Army of the Republic. It was deeded to the state in 1897. It's at California Dr. and Highway 29, Yountville.

No. 878: FIRST PRESBYTERIAN CHURCH BUILDING. It is considered an outstanding example of Victorian Gothic architectural styling. The church has been in continuous use since it construction in 1874. It's at 1333-3rd St., Napa.

No. 939: TWENTIETH CENTURY FOLK ART ENVIRONMENTS. This is one of California's exceptional Twentieth Century Folk Art Environments. Over a period of 30 years, Emanuele "Litto" Damonte collected more than 2,000 hubcaps. All around Hubcap Ranch are constructions and arrangements of hubcaps. See it at 6654 Pope Valley Rd., Pope Valley.

Nevada County

No. 134: DONNER MONUMENT. This monument commemorates the ill-fated Donner party of California-bound emigrants who were stranded here in 1846-47. Many died of exposure and starvation. It's located on Old Highway 40 at I-80 and Truckee Exit, Truckee.

No. 247: THE WORLD'S FIRST LONG DISTANCE PHONE LINE. This phone line was built in 1877 b y the Ridge Telephone Company. It connected French Corral with French Lake, a distance of 58 miles. It was operated by the Milton Mining Company from a building on this site that was built in 1853. It's on Pleasant Valley Road in the center of French Corral community.

No. 292: HOME OF LOLA MONTEZ. Lola was born in Limerick, Ireland July 3, 1818, as Maria Delores Eliza Rosanna Gilbert. Lola came to New York in 1851 and settled in Grass Valley in 1852. Mrs. Crabtree and her daughter Lotta met Lola Montez. They taught her how to sing and dance. It's located at 248 Mill St., Grass Valley.

No. 293: HOME OF LOTTA CRABTREE. Lotta Crabtree was born in New York in 1847. In 1852-3, gold fever brought her family to California. Several months after arriving in San Francisco, Mr. and Mrs. Crabtree and Lotta went to Grass Valley and started a boarding house for gold miners. It's located at 238 Mill St., Grass Valley.

No. 294: THE LITTLE TOWN OF ROUGH AND READY. The town was established in 1849 and named after General Zachary Taylor. In 1850, articles of secession were drawn up establishing the "Republic of Rough and Ready". As a result of disastrous fires, only a few buildings remain. It's at Highway 20 and Mountain Rose Rd., Rough and Ready.

No. 297: SITE OF ONE OF THE FIRST DISCOVERIES OF QUARTZ GOLD IN CALIFORNIA. It was here where the discovery of gold-bearing quartz was made and began quartz mining in California. The discovery was made on Gold Hill by George Knight in 1860. It's on the corner of Jenkins St. and Hocking Ave., Grass Valley.

No. 298: EMPIRE MINE. The Empire Mine was originally located by George D. Robert in 1850. In 1854, the Empire Mine was incorporated, and in 1865, new works, including a 30-stamp mill were erected. In 1869, it was purchased by William B. Bourn, Sr. When he died, William Bourn, Jr. took over its management. It's at Empire State Park.

No. 390: BRIDGEPORT (NYES CROSSING) COVERED BRIDGE. It was built in 1862 by David Isaac John Wood with lumber from his mill in Sierra County. The bridge was part of the Virginia Turnpike Company toll road which served the northern mines and the busy Nevada Comstock Lode. It is the longest covered bridge in the U.S. Its located on the west side of Pleasant Valley Road at the South Fork of the Yuba River, French Corral.

No. 628: ALPHA HYDRAULIC DIGGINGS. Located one mile north were the towns of Alpha and Omega, named by gold miners in the 1850s. The tremendous hydraulic diggings engulfed most of the original town sites. Alpha was the birthplace of famed opera singer Emma Nevada. It's located at Omega Rest Area, Highway 20.

No. 629: OMEGA HYDRAULIC DIGGINGS AND TOWNSITE. The tremendous hydraulic diggings engulfed most of the original town sites. Alpha was the birthplace of famed opera singer Emma Nevada. It's located at Omega Rest Area, Highway 20.

No. 780-6: FIRST CONTININENTAL RAILROAD-TRUCKEE. While construction on Sierra tunnels delayed Central Pacific, advance forces at Truckee began building 40 miles of track east and west of Truckee. The line reached Truckee April 3, 1868. Rails reached Reno June 19, and construction advanced eastward toward the meeting with Union Pacific. On May 10, 1861, the rails met at Promontory Point, Utah.

No. 799: OVERLAND EMIGRANT TRAIL. It is estimated that more than 30,000 people used this trail in 1849.

No. 832: SOUTH YUBA CANAL OFFICE. This was headquarters for the largest network of water flumes and ditches in the state. The South Yuba Canal Water Company was the first incorporated to supply water for hydraulic mining. A marker is located at 134 Main. St., Nevada City.

No. 843: NORTH STAR MINE POWERHOUSE. It was built in 1895 and the first complete plant of its kind. Compressed air, generated by Pelton water wheels, furnished power for the entire mine operation. See it at Pelton Wheel Museum, South Mill Road at Allison Ranch Road, Grass Valley.

No. 852: NORTH BLOOMFIELD MINING AND GRAVEL COMPANY. This was a major hydraulic mining operation. It boasted a vast system of canals and flumes. Its 7,800 foot drainage tunnel was termed a feat of engineering. The company was the principal defendant in an anti-debris lawsuit settled in 1884 in Judge Lorenzo Sawyer's court. The decision ended hydraulic mining.

No. 855: MOUNT SAINT MARY'S CONVENT AND ACADEMY. Under the Sisters of Mercy, it functioned as an academy 1868 to 1965 and as a convent from 1866 to 1868. It's at 5 Church St., Grass Valley.

No. 863: NEVADA THEATRE. It is California's oldest structure that existed as a theatre. It opened September 9, 1865. Celebrities such as Mark Twain, Jack London and Emma Nevada have appeared on its stage. It's at 401 Broad St., Nevada City.

No. 899: NATIONAL HOTEL. The National Exchange Hotel opened on August 20, 1856. The brick exterior is virtually unchanged. It is one of the oldest continuously operated hotels west of the Rockies. It's at 211 Broad St., Nevada City.

No. 914: HOLBROOKE HOTEL. It was built in 1862 around the Golden Gate Saloon. It's said to be an example of mid-19th century Mother Lode masonry structures. It's at 212 W. Main St., Grass Valley.

No. 1012: FIRST MANUFACTURRING SITE OF THE PELTON WHEEL. The Pelton Water Wheel was manufactured here at George Allan's Foundry and Machine Works. It was a major advancement in water power. It's at 325 Spring St., Nevada City.

Orange County

No. 112: NORTH GATE OF CITY OF ANAHEIM. A wall or fence of willow poles that took root and grew was planted around the Anaheim Colony to keep out the herds of wild cattle that roamed the surrounding country. Gates were erected at the north, east, south, and west ends of the two principal streets. It's located at 775 Anaheim Blvd. at North St., Anaheim.

No. 189: DANA POINT. It was named for Richard Henry Dana, author of "Two Years Before the Mast". El Embarcadero, in the cove below, was used by hide vessels trading with Mission San Juan Capistrano. In 1818, pirate Hipolito Bouchard, flying an Argentine flag, anchored his fleet here while raiding the mission.

No. 198: OLD LANDING. On September 10, 1870, Captain Samuel S. Dunnells and William A. Abbott opened Newport Bay to commerce when they entered it for the first time on the sternwheeler *Vaquero.*

No. 199: THE SERRANO ADOBE. Canada de los Alisos, also called El Toro, was granted to Jose Serrano in 1842 by Governor Juan Alvarado. Serrano built a number of adobes on the ranch, one of which still serves as private living quarters. It's at Lake Forest Dr. and Serrano Rd., El Toro.

No. 200: MISSION SAN JUAN CAPISTRANO. Founded in 1776 by Padre Junipero Serra, it is the seventh in the chain of 21 missions built in California. An earthquake destroyed the building in 1812.

No. 201: PIONEER HOUSE OF THE MOTHER COLONY. This was Anaheim's first house, built in 1857 by founder George Hanson. The Mother Colony was a German group that left San Francisco to form a grape-growing colony in Southern California. The vineyards, which became the largest in California, were destroyed by disease in 1885. The house is at 19111 Red Hill Road, Santa Ana.

No. 204: OLD SANTA ANA. Portola camped on the bank of the Santa Ana River in 1769. The place was designated Santa Ana by travelers and known by that name until the present town of Santa Ana was founded. It's at Lincoln Ave. and Orange Olive Rd., Orange.

No. 205: MODJESKA'S HOME. Famous as the home of Madame Modjeska, one of the world's greatest actresses, the house was designed by Stanford White in 1888. It's at Modjeska Canyon Rd. and Harding Canyon Rd., El Toro.

No. 217: BLACK STAR CANYON INDIAN VILLAGE SITE. The Indians who lived here stole some horses. White men followed them back to their camp. After a skirmish, the whites left with the horses the Indians had not already killed.

No. 218: BARTON MOUND. Juan Flores, who escaped from San Quentin, was sought by James Barton with a posse of five men. Near this mound, Flores surprised Barton and three of his men. All four were killed. Posses were formed and Flores and his men were captured. A marker is at I-405 and State Hwy 133, East Irvine.

No. 219: ANAHEIM LANDING. Soon after the founding of the Mother Colony at Anaheim in 1857, the Anaheim Landing Company established Anaheim Landing as a port for the Santa Ana Valley. It's at Seal Beach Blvd. and Electric Ave., Seal Beach.

No. 225: FLORES PEAK. In 1857, Juan Flores and a band of outlaws murdered Sheriff James Barton and part of his posse at Barton Mound. Pursued by a posse led by General Andres Pico, Flores and his men were finally caught on Flores Peak. It's located in the Tucker Wildlife Sanctuary.

No. 226: DON BERNARDO YORBA RANDHHOUSE SITE. Here, Bernardo Yorba created the greatest rancho of California's Golden Age. He combined the Santa Ana Grant, awarded to his father by the King of Spain, and the lands granted to him by Governor Jose Figueroa in 1834. The marker is at Esperanza Rd. and Echo Hill Ln., Yorba Linda.

No. 227: DIEGO SEPULVEDA HOUSE. This adobe house was built as a station of Mission San Juan Capistrano. It was used as a headquarters of Diego Sepulveda, owner of the rancho. It's at the corner of Mesa Verde Dr. and Adams Ave. Costa Meas.

No. 228: CARBONDALE. Coal was discovered here in 1878. The mine, called the Santa Clara, was operated by Southern Pacific. When the mine closed, Carbondale's buildings were moved away. It's located in Silverado.

No. 729: OLD MAIZELAND SCHOOL (RIVERA SCHOOL). It was built in 1868 and was the first school in the Rivera District. It's located at Knott's Berry Farm, Buena Park.

No. 775: SITE OF FIRST WATER-TO-WATER FLIGHT. On May 10, 1912, Glenn L. Martin flew his own plane, built in Santa Ana, from the waters of the Pacific Ocean at Balboa to Catalina Island. On his return trip, he carried the day's mail from Catalina, which was another first. It's at the end of Main St., Newport Beach.

No. 794: MCFADDEN WHARF. The original wharf was completed in 1888. As the seaward terminus of their Santa Ana and Newport Railway, it became the funnel through which flowed lumber and other goods that built the city of Orange.

No. 837: ORANGE COUNTY'S ORIGINAL COURTHOUSE. The structure was built in 1900 of Arizona red sandstone. It is the oldest existing courthouse in Southern California. Far-reaching court decisions have been handed down here, including the "Whipstock" case dealing with slant oil drilling, interpretation of farm labor law, and the Overell trial which resulted in law regulating explosives. It's at 211 W. Santa Ana Blvd., Santa Ana.

No. 918: OLINDA. From 1897, when oil pioneer Edward L. Doheny brought in the first well, to the 1940s, the boom town of Olinda sprawled over the surrounding hills. To the north was the Chanslor-Candfield Midway Oil Lease, and to the south, the Olinda Crude Oil lease. It's at 4442 Carbon Canyon Rd., Brea.

No. 959: BALBOA PAVILION. This is one of California's last surviving examples of great waterfront recreational pavilions from the turn of the century. It was built in 1905 by the Newport Bay Investment Company. It played a role in the development of Newport Beach as a seaside resort. It's at 400 Main St., Balboa.

No. 1004: OLDTOWN IRVINE. It stands as a testament to the rich agricultural past of one of California's most urban counties. All of these buildings have been rehabilitated for commercial uses and their exteriors have been painstakingly maintained. It's located at Sand Canyon Ave. and Burt Rd., Irvine.

No. 1015 RICHARD NIXON BIRTHPLACE. In 1912, Frank and Hannah Nixon built this modest farmhouse on their small citrus farm. Here, Richard Nixon was born, January 9, 1913. He was the 37th President of the United States. It's located at 18061 Yorba Linda Blvd., Yorba Linda.

Placer County

No. 397: TOWN OF DUTCH FLAT. It was founded by Joseph and Charles Dornback in 1851. Dutch Flat was noted for its rich hydraulic mines. In 1860, it had the largest voting population in Placer County.

No. 398: YANKEE JIM'S. Gold was discovered here in 1850 by "Yankee Jim", a reputed lawless character. The first mining ditch in California was constructed here. It's located in Foresthill.

No. 399: TOWN OF FORESTHILL. Gold was discovered here in 1850. In 1852, the Jenny Lind Mine produced more than one million dollars in gold. The marker is at 24540 Main St., Forest Hill.

No. 400: VIRGINIATOWN. It was commonly called Virginia. More than 2,000 miners worked the rich deposits here. In 1852, Captain John Brislow built California's first railroad to carry pay dirt one mile to Auburn Ravine. It was the site of Philip Armour;s and George Aldrich's butcher shop, which led to the founding of the Chicago Armour meatpacking company. A marker is at Fowler and Virginiatown roads, Newcastle.

No. 401: IOWA HILL. The total production of gold from Iowa Hill has been placed at twenty million dollars. The town was destroyed by fire in 1857 and again in 1862. Each time it was rebuilt, but the last big fire in 1922 destroyed most of the town. A marker is near the post office, Iowa Hill.

No. 402: TOWN OF MICHIGAN BLUFF. When it was founded in 1950, it was known as Michigan City. Leland Stanford operated a store in Michigan City from 1853 to 1855. In 1858, the town was undermined and became unsafe. It was moved to its present site and called Michigan Bluff.

No. 403: EMIGRANT GAP. When the first covered wagons came over the Sierra Nevada in the spring of 1845, they turned westward to Emigrant Gap. There, the wagons were lowered by ropes to the floor of Bear Valley. The marker is at Emigrant Gap Vista Point.

No. 404: CITY OF AUBURN. Gold was discovered here by Claude Chana on May 16, 1848. The place was first known as "North Fork" or "Woods Dry Diggins". The settlement was given the name Auburn in 1849. It became the county seat of Sutter County in 1850 and of Placer County in 1851. A marker is at the corner of Maple St. and Lincoln Way.

No. 405: TOWN OF GOLD RUN. Gold Run was famous for its hydraulic mines. It shipped $6,125,000 in gold from 1865 to 1878. A plaque is across the street from the post office.

No. 463 OPHIR. It was founded in 1849 as Spanish Corral. It received its Biblical name in 1850 because of its rich placers. It was the most populace town Placer County in 1852, polling 500 votes. It was almost totally destroyed by fire in 1853, but made a comeback as a quartz mining center. A marker is on corner of Lozanos and Bald Hill Rds., Auburn.

No. 585: PIONEER EXPRESS TRAIL. Pioneer Express riders rode this gold rush trail to the many populous mining camps on the American River bars that are now covered by Folsom Lake. A marker is at Folsom Lake State Recreation Area, Folsom.

No. 724: PIONEER SKI AREA OF AMERICA, SQUAW VALLEY. The VIII Olympic Winter Games of 1960 commemorated a century of sport skiing in California. The Sierra Nevada began seeing the first organized ski clubs. Check the marker at the Lobby Entrance of Cable Car Building in Squaw Valley.

No. 170-1: FIRST TRANSCONTINENTAL RAILOAD-ROSEVILLE. Central Pacific graders arrived at junction November 23, 1863. When the track reached there April 25, 1864, trains began making the 18-mile run to and from Sacramento daily. Junction is now called Roseville, which became a major railroad distribution center. A marker is at corner of Church and Washington Streets.

No. 780-2: FIRST TRANSCONTINENTAL RAILROAD-ROCKLIN. The Central Pacific reached Rocklin in May 1864. Trains moving over the Sierra were generally cut into two sections at this point in order to ascend the grade. The terminal was moved to Roseville in 1908. Marker is at Rocklin Road and First St., Rocklin.

No. 780-3 FIRST TRANSCONTINENTAL RAILROAD-NEWCASTLE. Regular freight and passenger trains began operating over the first 31 miles of Central Pacific's line to Newcastle June 10, 1864. Marker at Main and Page Sts., Newcastle.

No. 780-4: FIRST TRANSCONTINENTAL RAILROAD-AUBURN. After an 11-month delay due to political opposition and lack of money, Central Pacific tracks reached Auburn May 13. 1865. The marker is at 639 Lincoln Way, Auburn.

No. 780-5 FIRST TRANSCONTINENTAL RAILROAD-FAIRFAX. The town was called Illinois-town in 1865. Governor Leland Stanford renamed it Colfax in honor of Schuyler Colfax, Speaker of the House of Representatives. For the railroads, the real assault on the Sierra began here. Marker is at Grass Valley Street and Railroad tracks, Colfax.

No. 707: LAKE TAHOE OUTLET GATES. Conflicting control of these gates, first built in 1870, resulted in the two-decade "Tahoe Water War" between lakeshore owners and downstream Truckee River water users. The dispute was settled in 1910-11 when a technique for determining water content in snow was developed. Marker is at the corner of the Truckee River bridge.

No. 799-2: OVERLAND EMIGRANT TRAIL. Rocks near this site still bear the marks of wagon wheels of pioneer wagons on their way to the gold fields. The next ordeal was the tortuous descent into Bear Valley. Wagons were lowered by ropes to the floor of the valley. Marker is at the Ranger Station, Soda Springs.

No. 885: GRIFFITH QUARRY. This quarry was established in 1864 by Griffith Griffith, a native of Wales. This quarry supplied high-quality granite for important building in San Francisco and Sacramento. Marker is on Taylor and Rock Springs Rd., Penryn.

Plumas County

No. 184: PETER LASSEN MARKER. In the summer of 1850, Peter Lassen and a companion, Isidore Meyerwitz, went to Indian Valley and selected a suitable location for a ranch. They erected a log cabin in 1851 to house their trading post. Lassen then moved to Honey Valley in 1855. He was killed from ambush while prospecting in 1859. A marker is on North Valley Road, east of Greenville.

No. 196: JAMISON CITY, EUREKA MILLS, JOHNSTOWN, AND THE FAMOUS EUREKA MINE. Along the Pioneer Trail lies Jamison City and mine, the large producer of the famous 52-pound nugget. Eureka Mill and mine yielded $17 million to Cornish miners and others. The marker is at Plumas-Eureka State Park.

No. 197: BUCK'S LAKE. This was the site of a ranch established by Horace Bucklin and Francis Walker in 1850. It later became a hotel, post office, and express office. Marker is at Buck's Lake Lodge Marina.

No. 212: PIONEER GRAVE (GRIZZLY CREEK) Legend says a lad was returning to Marysville with a load of provisions for the mines. He was murdered and robbed. Later a comrade carved his name, age. etc. on a tree. It read: Peter Linthiouh died September, 1852, age 19. Marker is on Buck's Lake Road.

No. 213: RABBIT CREEK HOTEL MONUMENT. Laporte, first known as Rabbit Creek, was one of the most important settlements in the southern part of Plumas County. In the fall of 1852, Eli S. Lester built the Rabbit Creek Hotel. Marker is on corner of Main and Church Streets, Laporte.

No. 231: ELIZABETHTOWN. Tate's Ravine was named in the spring of 1852. Alex and Frank Tate discovered gold there. A rich mine opened up and the miners wanted a different name for their town. They named it Elizabethtown in honor of miner Lewis Clark's daughter.

No. 336: BECKWOURTH'S PASS. Beckwourth's Pass is at an elevation of 5,221 feet. It is the lowest pass in the Sierra Nevada. It was discovered by James Beckwourth in 1851. A marker is at a roadside rest area in Chilcoot.

337: RICH BAR": Gold was found here in July 1850 by miners coming from the Yuba Diggins. There was considerable production during the early 1850s. The Rich Bar marker is on State Highway 70 23.6 miles northwest of Quincy.

No. 479: SITE OF AMERICAN RANCH AND HOTEL. James H. Bradley built the hotel in 1854 in Quincy. Three commissioners met there March 18, 1854, to form a new county from a portion of Butte County. A marker is located at 355 Main St., Quincy.

No. 480 : SITE OF PLUMAS HOUSE. The first and second Plumas Houses were built on this site. The second one was built in 1866 by James and Jane Edwards. This hotel was the center of Quincy's social and business life for more than 30 years. The hotel burned to the ground in 1923. Check for a marker on Main and Court Sts., Quincy.

No. 481: SPANISH RANCH AND MEADOW VALLEY. Miners going to the East Branch, Middle Fork, or North Fork of the Feather River separated at Spanish Rancho. The rancho was built in 1850 by two Spaniards. A marker is on a Spanish Ranch side road.

No. 625: PIONEER SCHOOLHOUSE. In 1857, residents at the eastern end of American Valley built a school. It was the first schoolhouse in Plumas County. Mr. S.A. Ballou was engaged as teacher for 19 children. Marker is on the Quincy County Fairgrounds.

No. 723: PIONEER SKI AREA OF AMERICA, JOHNSVILLE. The first sport ski area in the western hemisphere was in the Sierra Nevada. By 1860 races were being held in the Plumas-Sierra region. A marker is in front of the Museum at Plumas-Eureka State Park.

Riverside County

No. 20: PARENT WASHINGTON NAVEL ORANGE TREE. This tree was introduced into the United States from Bahia, Brazil. There were 12 young trees received and buds from them were propagated on sweet orange seedlings. In 1873, two of these greenhouse-grown trees were sent to Mrs. Eliza Tibbetts in Riverside. It is said the reason for the tree's healthy growth was its daily dashing with dishwater. A marker is located at Magnolia and Arlington Sts., Riverside.

No. 101: GIANT DESERT FIGURES. The times of origin and meaning of these giant figures remains a mystery. The largest of these figures is 167 feet long and the smallest is 95 feet. There are three figures, two of animals and one of a coiled serpent. They're on Highway 95, 16 miles north of Blythe.

No. 102: SITE OF LOUIS RUBIDOUX HOUSE. In 1844, Louis Rubidoux arrived in California, his family coming shortly after. He purchased the Jurupa Rancho. Rubidoux became one of the most prosperous stock raisers in Southern California. It's in the 5575 block, Mission Blvd., Rubidoux.

No. 103: SITE OF DE ANZA CAMP, MARCH 1774. Juan Bautista de Anza, an explorer and colonizer, led the first non-Indian explorers to cross the mountains into California through this pass. In the party were Spaniards from Sonora, who became the founders of San Francisco. A marker is at 60901 Coyote Canyon Road, Anza.

No. 104: SITE OF INDIAN VILLAGE OF POCHEA. Pochea was one of a cluster of Indian villages forming the very large settlement of Pahsitnah. It extended along the ridge east and west of Romona Bowl. Pahsitnah was thriving when the Spanish first passed in 1774. A tragic story tells of the natives contracting smallpox from Europeans. A terrible epidemic spread and some survivors fled the area to Soboba Reservation. A marker has been placed at Ramona Bowl, 27400 Girard St., Hemet.

No. 185: SERRANO BOULDER. Don Leandro Serrano had cattle, sheep, cultivated land and orchards in the Temescal Valley. A boulder was placed by residents of Temescal Valley to mark the site of the first house in Riverside County. A marker has been placed about nine miles south of Corona.

No. 186: SERRANO TANNING VATS. Two vats, built in 1819 by the Luiseno Indians, were used in making leather from cow hides. The vats were restored in 1981 and placed here by the Billy Holcomb Chapter of E Clampus Vitus. Marker is at 1-15 and Old Temescal Rd.

No. 187l: CARVED ROCK. These petroglyphs were carved by the Luiseno Indians. Their meaning is said to be "A chief died here." The carvings are his plumes, his portrait, his sign, and the animals are sacred to him. The rock has been damaged by vandals. It's eight miles south of Corona.

No. 188: BUTTERFIELD STAGE STATION. This is where mail was delivered and horses changed. The first stagecoach left Tipton, Missouri on September 15, 1858 and, passing through Temescal, arrived in Los Angeles October 7, 1858. Marker is at 20730 Temescal Road, south of Corona.

No. 190: PAINTED ROCK. Santa Fe Railroad has preserved this rock with its ancient pictograph, and the Corona Women's Improvement Club has placed a tablet. Marker is seven miles south of Corona.

No. 224: RUINS OF THIRD SERRANO ADOBE: Dono Leandreo Serrano set out orchards and vineyards and cultivated some of the fertile lands of the Temescal Valley in the 1840s. He built a third adobe which the Serrano family occupied until 1898. A marker is on I-15 and Old Temescal Road.

No. 303: SITE OF OLD RUBIDOUX GRIST MILL. It was one of the first grist mills in this part of Southern California. It was built on Rancho Jurupa in 1846-47. Marker is at 5540 Molina Way, Rubidoux.

No. 557: HEMET MAZE STONE. This pictograph is an outstanding example of the work of prehistoric peoples. A marker is located at Maze Stone Park, Hemet.

No. 638: OLD TEMECAL ROAD. This route was used by Luiseno and Gabrieleno Indians, whose villages were nearby. It was the southern emigrant road for gold seekers from1849 to 1851. It was used by Overland Mail Route 1858 to 1861. Marker is on Old Highway 71.

No. 738: CORONA FOUNDERS MONUMENT: The Citrus Colony and Town of Corona were founded on May 4, 1886. Marker is at 100 block of 6th Street, Corona.

No. 749: SAAHATPA: Chief Juan Antonio and his band of Cahuilla Indians helped white settlers in the San Bernardino area defend their property against outlaws during the 1840s. A monument marker has been placed at Brookside Rest Area.

No. 761: MISSION INN. Frank A. Miller made the adobe bricks for a small 12-room guest house that he opened in 1876. Over the years he added to the Building. Marker is at 7th and Orange. Riverside.

No. 787: DE ANZA CROSSING OF THE SANTA ANA RIVER. The first party of colonists to come overland to the Pacific Coast crossed the Santa Ana River and camped here. These emigrants continued their journey north and founded the City of San Francisco. Marker is near Union Pacific Bridge.

No. 943: CORNELIUS AND MERCEDES JENSON RANCH: Danish sea captain Cornelius Jenson sailed to San Francisco during the Gold Rush to sell his cargo. He settled in Agua Mansa, established a store and married Mercedes Alvarado. It's located at 4350 Riverview Dr., Rubidoux.

No. 948: SITE OF BLYTHE INTAKE. On July 17, 1877, Thomas Blythe, a San Francisco financier filed the first legal claim for Colorado River water rights. Oliver Callaway planned a diversion dam and canal which opened in 1877 to irrigate the Palo Verde Valley. Marker is on U.S. 95 north of Blythe.

No. 985: DESERT TRAINING CENTER. General George S. Patton established three training centers, one at Camp Young, the second at Camp Coxcomb and a third at Camp Granite. All were used to train troops during World War II. Markers are at General Patton Memorial Museum, Chiraco summit, Indio, and at Desert Center.

No. 989: SOVIET TRANSPOLAR LANDING SITE: Three Soviet aviators completed a transpolar flight from Moscow in 62 hours. Marker is at Cottonwood and Sanderson Sts., San Jacinto.

No. 992: SITE OF CONTRACTOR'S GENERAL HOSPITAL. In 1933, Dr. Sidney R. Garfield opened Contractor's General Hospital 6 miles west of Desert Center. The hospital treated workers on the Colorado River Aqueduct through a prepaid insurance plan. Marker is located next to Post Office, Desert Center.

No. 1005: SANTA ROSA RANCHO: Santa Rosa Rancho is considered a prime example of various historical phases of cattle ranching. A marker is at 22115 Tenaja Road, Murieta.

No. 1009: RAMONA BOWL, SITE OF THE RAMONA PAGEANT. Helen Hunt Jackson's historical novel, "Ramona" is brought to life each year in this presentation. Marker is at 27400 Ramona Bowl Rd., Hemet.

Sacramento County

No. 366: PIONEER TELEGRAPH STATION. Erroneously called the Pony Express Terminal, this location was occupied by the State Telegraph Company 1863-1868 and the Western Union Telegraph Company, 1868-1915. Marker is at 1015 2nd St., Old Sacramento.

No. 439: SITE OF GRIST MILL BUILT BY JARED DIXON SHELDON. Jared Sheldon built the mill on Omochumnes Rancho. The rancho was granted to him by the Mexican government in 1823. Sheldon was shot in a quarrel over a dam he built that flooded miners' claims. A marker is at Prairie City and State Highway 50.

No. 464: PRAIRIE CITY. This was a mining town and center of trade during gold rush days. Prairie City included 15 stores and 10 boarding houses and hotels. Two stage lines operated daily. See the marker at corner of Prairie City Road and State Highway 50.

No. 468: MICHIGAN BAR: It's been almost obliterated by hydraulic mining. Gold was discovered here by citizens of Michigan. Marker is on Highway 16.

No. 525: SUTTER'S FORT. John Augustus Sutter founded the fort in 1839 to protect his 76-square mile Mexican land grant. The walls, which disappeared by the 1860s, were rebuilt after the State acquired the property in 1890. Marker is at 27th and L Sts., Sacramento.

No. 526: CALIFORNIA'S FIRST PASSENGER RAILROAD. The Sacramento Valley Railroad, running from Sacramento to Folsom, began February 12, 1855. Marker is at corner of 3rd and R Streets, Sacramento.

No. 558: TERMINAL OF CALIFORNIA'S FIRST PASSENGER RAILROAD. Completion of the Sacramento Valley Railroad in 1856 was celebrated by enthusiastic residents of both Sacramento and Folsom. Marker is in Leidesdorff Plaza, Folsom.

No. 566: SACRAMENTO CITY CEMETERY. Many of the victims of the cholera epidemic of 1850 are buried here. The cemetery includes many of Sacramento's founders and governors. See the marker at Broadway and 10th Streets, Sacramento.

No. 575: SLOUGHHOUSE. This was a prominent hotel and stage station on the road to the Amador mines. It was built by Jared Dixon Sheldon, but destroyed by fire in 1890. It was rebuilt the same year. Marker is at Meiss St. and Highway 16, Sloughhouse.

No. 591: SUTTER'S LANDING. Captain John A. Sutter landed approximately 200 feet north of here when he arrived in 1839. Sutter and his men were the first non-Indian settlers within the present city limits of Sacramento. Marker is corner of 28th and C Streets., Sacramento.

No. 592: NEW HELVETIA CEMETERY. This was the site of Sacramento's first cemetery. Marker is at Alhambra Blvd. and J Street, Sacramento.

No. 593: SUTTERVILLE. This is where Sutter laid out his townsite in 1844. See marker on Sutterville Road.

No. 594: SITE OF CHINA SLOUGH. The site of the slough which formerly extended from Third to Fifth streets, is now occupied by the Southern Pacific Depot. A marker is on Fourth and I streets, Sacramento.

No. 595: EAGLE THEATER. This is the site of the first building in California constructed as a theater in 1849. Marker is in Old Sacramento State Park.

No. 596: SITE OF HOME OF NEWTON BOOTH. Newton Booth was the Governor of California 1871-1873 and U.S. Senator 1873-1879. Marker is at 1015-17 Front St., Sacramento.

No. 597: WHAT CHEER HOUSE. This celebrated hotel was built in 1853. State offices were here in 1855. A marker is at Front and K Streets, Sacramento.

No.598: SITE OF STAGE AND RAILROAD. This is the site of the terminal of stages of the 1850s and the Sacramento Railroad in 1955. A marker is in Old Sacramento State Park.

No. 599: E.B. CROCKER ART GALLERY. It was erected in 1870 to house the private collection of Judge and E.B. Crocker. A marker is at 216 O St., Sacramento.

No. 600: HEADQUARTERS OF THE BIG FOUR. This landmark has been retired and this landmark site is included in Old Sacramento Landmark No. 812.

No. 601: WESTERN HOTEL. The hotel was built by William Land in 1875. It was one of the largest in the West. A marker is at 2nd and K streets.

No. 602: EBNER'S HOTEL. This hotel was built by Charles Ebner in 1856. Captain Sutter was a frequent visitor. See marker at 116 ½ K St., Old Sacramento.

No. 603: LADY ADAMS BUILDING. This store and office building was built in 1852. Materials for the building were brought around the Horn. Marker is at 117-119 K St., Old Sacramento.

No. 604: SITE OF THE SAM BRANNON HOUSE. The building was erected in 1853 by Henry Robinson on land owned by Sam Brannon. It was used as the first meeting place of the Pioneer Association. Marker is at 112 J. Street, Old Sacramento.

No. 605: SITE OF SACRAMENTO UNION. This building was occupied by the Sacramento Union in the 1850s. Marker is at 121 J. Street, Old Sacramento.

No. 606: B.F. HASTINGS BUILDING. Erected in 1852-53, this building was occupied by B.F. Hastings Bank, Wells Fargo & Co. The first journey eastward of the Pony Express was begun here in April 4, 1860. A marker is at 1000 Second St., Old Sacramento.

No. 607: ADAMS AND COMPANY BUILDING. It was built in 1853 and occupied by the Adams and Co. express and banking house. A marker is at 1014 Second Street, Old Sacramento.

No. 608: SITE OF ORLEANS HOTEL. The hotel was built in 1852. It served as a depot for stage companies. A marker is at 1018 Second St., Old Sacramento.

No. 609: D.O. MILLS BANK BUILDING. Built in 1852, the building housed one of the oldest and largest banks of early-day California. Marker is 100 feet from corner of Second and J Streets, Old Sacramento.

No. 610: OVERTON BUILDING. Built in 1852, it was occupied by various state offices. Marker is located at Second and J Streets, Old Sacramento.

No. 611: ORIGINAL SACRAMENTO BEE BUILDING. The Sacramento Bee was founded in 1857. Its early home was in this building. A marker is on the West side of Third Street.

No. 612: SITE OF PIONEER MUTUAL VOLUNTEER FIREHOUSE. Built in 1854, it was occupied by Engine Co. No. 1, the oldest fire company in California. A marker is at Third and J Streets, Old Sacramento.

No. 613: SITE OF CONGREGATIONAL CHURCH. In 1849, Rev. Joseph A. Benton organized the church in Sacramento. Marker is at 915 Sixth St., Sacramento.

No. 614: STANFORD-LATHROP HOME. Designed by Seth Babson in 1857, it was purchased by Leland Stanford in 1861. Jane Lathrop Stanford gave the house to the Roman Catholic Diocese of Sacramento. A marker is at 800 N. St, Sacramento.

No. 633: OLD FOLSOM POWERHOUSE. Horatio Gates Livermore pioneered the development of ditches and dams on the American River for industry and agriculture. Find the marker at Folsom Powerhouse State Park.

No. 654: SITE OF THE FIRST JEWISH SYNAGOGUE OWNED BY CONGREGATION ON THE PACIFIC COAST. The building was prefabricated in Baltimore and shipped around Cape Horn in 1849. It housed the Methodist Episcopal Church until sold in 1852. Marker is in sidewalk, Seventh Street.

No. 654-1: CHEVRA KADDISHA (HOME OF PEACE CEMETERY) This was the first Jewish cemetery in California. Marker is at 3230 St. Sacramento.

No. 657: GRAVE OF ALEXANDER HAMILTON WILLARD. He was the last survivor of the exploring party sent out by President Jefferson to discover the course and source of the Missouri River. Marker is in Franklin Cemetery, Franklin.

No. 666: CAMP UNION, SUTTERVILLE. The 5th Infantry Regiment, California Volunteers, was trained by Brevet Brigadier George W. Bowie for duty against Confederate forces in Arizona, New Mexico and Texas. Marker is at corner of Susanville and Land Park Dr., Sacramento.

No. 680: MURPHYS RANCH. This is where the U.S. began its conquest of California. In 1846, American settlers, led by Ezekial Merritt overpowered Mexican soldiers and took their horses. The Bear Flag Revolt followed. A marker is on Grant Line Road and Highway 99, Elk Grove.

No. 697: FIVE MILE HOUSE-OVERLAND PONY EXPRESS ROUTE IN CALIFORNIA. In 1860, Sam (Bill) Hamilton carried the first mail of the Central Overland Pony Express from here. Marker is at California State University, 6000 J Street Sacramento.

No. 698: FIFTEEN MILE HOUSE-OVERLAND PONY EXPRESS ROUTE IN CALIFORNIA. This was the site of the second remount station of the Central Overland Pony Express. Sam "Bill" Hamilton carried the first eastward mail from here. Marker is at White Rock and Gold Valley Roads, Rancho Cordova.

No. 702: FOLSOM-OVERLAND PONY EXPRESS ROUTE IN CALIFORNIA. This was the western terminus for the Central Overland Pony Express. Marker can be seen at 819 Sutter St.

No. 719: GRAVE OF ELITHA CUMI DONNER WILDER. She was the daughter of George and Mary Blue Donner. She was rescued by the first relief party to reach the scene. A marker is located at Elk Grove Masonic Cemetery.

No. 745: THE COLOMA ROAD-SUTTER'S FORT. This road was used by James Marshall to bring news of his gold discovery to John Sutter. The discovery marked the start of the California gold rush. A marker is at 28th and L streets, Sacramento.

No. 746: COLOMA ROAD-NIMBUS DAM. This road was used by James Marshall to bring the first gold from Sutter's Mill to Sutter's Fort. The road was later traveled by thousands of gold seekers. Marker is at Folsom Lake State Recreation Area.

No. 780: FIRST TRANSCONTINENTAL RAILROAD: This was the start of the First Transcontinental Railroad on January 8, 1863. The railroad was completed six years later. A marker can be found in Old Sacramento State Historic Park.

No. 780-8: FIRST TRANSCONTINENTAL RAILROAD-WESTERN BASE OF THE SIERRA NEVADA. President Abraham Lincoln decreed that the western base of the Sierra Nevada began where the Central Pacific Railroad crossed Arcade Creek. A marker is at Haggin Oaks Golf Course at 3645 Fulton, Sacramento.

No. 812: OLD SACAMENTO. Founded in 1848 by John Sutter, Jr., Sacramento was an outgrowth of Sutter's Fort. It's located between J and L streets.

No. 817: SITE OF FIRST COUNTY FREE LIBRARY BRANCH IN CALIFORNIA. Through the efforts of Miss Harriet G. Eddy, principal of Elk Grove Union High School, Elk Grove acquired the first county free library branch. Marker is at 9125 Elk Grove Blvd., Elk Grove.

No. 823: GOVERNOR'S MANSION. This Victorian house was built in 1877. It was acquired by the state for the residence of Governor George C. Pardee. The Pardee family moved in in 1903. Marker is at 16th and H Sts., Sacramento.

No. 869: SITE OF FIRST AND SECOND STATE CAPITOLS AT SACRAMENTO. Sacramento's first county courthouse at this site served as the State's Capitol from January 16, 1852 until May 4, 1852 and from March 1, 1854 to May 15, 1854. Marker is at Seventh and L streets, Sacramento.

No. 872: CALIFORNIA'S CAPITOL COMPLEX. The historic Capitol was designed by architects M.F. Butler and Ruben Clark. Work began in 1860 and by late 1869, the Capitol was partly occupied. A marker is located at the intersection Tenth Street and Capitol Mall, Sacramento.

No. 900: NISIPOWINAN VILLAGE SITE. This was the site of the most significant Indian Village and cemetery in this region. Address is restricted per Section 6254.10 of the California State Code.

No. 934. TEMPORARY DETENTION CAMPS FOR JAPANESE AMERICANS-SACRAMENTO ASSEMBLY CENTER. These facilities were intended to confine Japanese until more permanent concentration camps could be built. Marker is located in Walerga Park, Sacramento.

No. 967: CALIFORNIA ALMOND GROWERS EXCHANGE. The exchange was formed in 1910 as the first grower-owned cooperative. The first structure was built in 1915 and was designed to mechanize almond processing.

No. 991: STATE INDIAN MUSEUM. This museum was built as the first state-run museum devoted to Indian culture. A marker is at 2618 K Street, Sacramento.

No. 1013: SITE OF THE FIRST AFRICAN AMERICAN CHURCH ESTABLISHED ON THE PACIFIC COAST. This is the first church building associated with an African American religious congregation on the Pacific Coast. A marker is at 715 Seventh St., Sacramento.

San Benito County

No. 179: CASTRO HOUSE. Castro House was built to house General Jose Castro's administrative office and his secretary in the 1840s. It was sold to Patrick Breen, a survivor of the Donner Party. A marker is at San Juan Bautista Park.

No. 180: PLAZA HOTEL. Angelo Zanetta added a second story to this one-story adobe barracks in 1858. It was built to house soldiers and operated for many years. See the marker at San Juan Bautista State Historic Park.

No. 181: FREMONT PEAK. John Charles Fremont built a fort here on Gabilan Peak. He waited for four days for the attack of Californios. The battle did not materialize. A marker is located in Abbey Park at Second and Mariposa Sts.

No. 195: MISSION SAN JUAN BAUTISTA AND PLAZA. It was founded in 1790 and then destroyed by earthquakes of 1800 and 1906. The two bells it now uses were salvaged from its original chime. A marker is at Second and Mariposa Streets, San Juan Bautista.

No. 324: NEW IDRIA MINE. It was named for New Idria mine in Austria. It's one of the most famous quicksilver mines of the world. See the marker at New Idria Mine Road.

San Bernardino County

No. 42: SAN BERARDINO ASISTENCIA. This branch of San Gabriel Mission was built about 1830 on the San Bernardino Rancho. After the rancho's sale to the Mormons, it was occupied by Bishop Tenney. A marker is at 26930 Barton Rd., Redlands.

No. 43: THE ZANJA: Spanish missionaries introduced the principle of irrigation in San Bernardino Valley. Franciscan fathers engineered and Indians dug the first ditch or "zanja". A marker is at Sylvan Park, University St. Redlands.

No. 44: SITE OF THE MORMON STOCKADE. In 1851, a stockade of logs was built here as protection against Indians. More than 100 families lived in it for more than a year. A marker is located at the San Bernardino County Courthouse, Arrowhead and Court Street, San Bernardino.

No. 95: GUACHAMA RANCHERIA. The Guachama Rancheria was renamed San Bernardino by Francisco Dumetz. A marker can be found at 25894 Mission Road, Redlands.

No. 96: MORMON ROAD. When the Mormons came to San Bernardino Valley in 1851, they needed suitable lumber to construct homes and a stockade. They built a wagon road into the San Bernardino Mountains. A marker is in Waterman Canyon.

No. 121: AGUA MANSA. Don Bandini, owner of Jurupa Rancho, donated parts of his rancho to a group of New Mexican colonists in 1845 on the understanding that they would aid in repelling Indian raids on his stock. The community was named Agua Mansa (Gentle Water). A marker is at the Agua Mansa Cemetery, 270 E. Agua Mansa Rd., Colton.

No. 191: YORBA-SLAUGHTER ADOBE. This adobe was built in 1850 by Raimundo Yorba. It was purchased from him by Fenton Mercer Slaughter in 1868. A marker is at 17127 Pomona-Rincon Road, Chino.

No. 360: TAPIA ADOBE. In 1839, Governor Juan Alvarado granted the 13,000-acre tract called Cucamonga to Tiburcio Tapia, an ex-soldier. A marker is located at 8916 Foothill Blvd., Cucamonga.

No. 490: CUCMONGA RANCHO WINERY. This winery was established by Tiburcio Tapia. A marker is located at 8916 Foothill Blvd., Cucamonga.

No. 528: YUCAIPA ADOBE. It was built 1842 by Diego Sepulveda. It is believed to be the oldest house in San Bernardino County. A marker is located at 32183 Kentucky St., Yucaipa.

No. 573: SYCAMORE GROVE. The Sycamore Valley Ranch was formerly called Sycamore Grove. It was the first camp of the Mormon pioneers. A marker is at Glen Helen Regional Park, 2555 Devore Road, Devore.

No. 576: SANTA FE AND SALT LAKE TRAIL MONUMENT. This monument was erected in 1917 in honor of the 500 Mormon pioneers who came through the pass to the San Bernardino Valley. A marker is at W. Cajon Canyon on State Highway 138l.

No. 578: STODDARD-WAITE MONUMENT. This monument marks the western extension of the Santa Fe Trail traveled by Sheldon Stoddard and Sydney P. Waite in 1849. A marker is located at Elsie Arey May Nature Center, San Bernardino.

No. 579: DALEY TOLL ROAD MONUMENT. The Daley Road was built by Edward Daley in 1870. It was one of the first roads into the San Bernardino Mountains that could accommodate wagons. A marker is located on State Highway 18.

No.617: FORT BENSON: This fortification was built in 1856-57 by the independent faction in a dispute with the Mormons over a land title. A marker can be found at 10600 Hunts Lane, Colton.

No. 618: GARCES-SMITH MONUMENT. This monument marks an old Indian trail, the Mojave Trail, used by Father Garces in March 1776. Call the Cajon Ranger District for permission to view the plaque.

No. 619: HOLCOMB VALLEY. Southern California's richest gold rush followed the discovery of rich placer deposits. A marker is located Belleville Holcomb Valley, on Road 3N16.

No. 620: YUCAIPA RANCHERIA. Yucaipa Valley supported a large population of Serrano Indians. The Indians called this area *Yucaipat* (wet lands). A marker is at 32183 Kentucky St., Yucaipa.

No. 622: HARRY WADE EXIT ROUTE. After getting to Death Valley with an ill-fated caravan, Harry Wade found this exit route for his ox-drawn wagon, saving his life and the lives of his wife and children. A monument exists 4 miles south of Death Valley National Monument.

No. 717: THE ANGELES NATIONAL FOREST. It was the first national forest in California and the second in the United State. The first name given to the forest was "San Gabriel Timberland Reserve". A marker is at Clear Creek vista point, La Canada.

No. 725: OLD BEAR VALLEY DAM. In 1884, Frank Brown built an unusual dam to supply irrigation water for the Redlands area. It was a single-arch granite dam that formed Big Bear Lake. It was then the world's largest man-made dam. Engineers claimed the dam would not hold, and declared it the "Eighth Wonder of the World" when it did hold. A marker can be found on the West edge of Big Bear Lake.

No. 737: CHIMNEY ROCK: Conflicts between Indians and white settlers over the rich lands of the San Bernardino Mountains culminated in the battle at Chimney Rock. The Indians were forced to retreat to the desert. A marker is on Rabbit Springs Road, Lucerne Valley.

No. 774: SEARLES LAKE BORAX DISCOVERY: John Searles discovered borax on the surface of Searles Lake in 1862. He and his brother, Dennis, formed the San Bernardino Borax Mining Company in 1873. A marker is located at the roadside rest in Trona.

No. 781: NATIONAL OLD TRAILS MONUMENT. An old Indian trail, still visible in some places, ran roughly parallel to the Colorado River on the California side. Garces and his Mojave guides and Jedediah Smith used the route in 1826. A marker is located at the Colorado River Bridge, Needles.

No. 782: TOWN OF CALICO. The Calico Mining District had a peak population of 3,000. The district produced between $13 and $20 million in silver and $9 million in borate minerals between 1881 and 1907. A marker is four miles northwest of Ghost Town Road on Highway I-15 at Yermo.

No. 782: VON SCHMIDT STATE BOUNDARY MONUMENT, This cast-iron column was erected in 1873. It marks the southern terminus of the California-Nevada State boundary established by A. W. Von Schmidt's 1872-73 survey. Von Schmidt's line was the first officially recognized oblique state line between California and Nevada. A marker is Pew Road, Needles.

No. 892: HARVEY HOUSE. In 1893, Fred Harvey, founder and operator of the Santa Fe Harvey Houses, took over operation of all hotel and restaurants on the Santa Fe line. A marker is located at Santa Fe Depot, First Ave and Riverside Dr. Barstow.

No. 939: TWENTIETH CENTURY FOLK ART ENVIRONMENT-POSSUM TROT. Isaac Williams built a large adobe on the 22,000-acre Rancho Chino. The "Battle of Chino" occurred at the adobe September 26-27, 1846 when 24 Americans were captured by a group 50 Californios. A marker is located at the Chino Fire Station, Chino.

No. 950: UNITED STATES RABBIT EXPERIMENT STATION. Here, the United States established the first and only station devoted to research on the breeding and raising of rabbits. A marker is at 8384 Cypress Ave, Fontana.

No. 963: THE MOJAVE ROAD. In 1826, explorer Jedediah Smith used the Mohave Indians paths to reach the California Coast overland from mid-America. A marker is at Midway Rest Area, Barstow.

No. 963-1: CAMP CADY (ON THE MOJAVE TRAIL) Camp Cady was established by U.S. Dragoons in 1860 to protect travelers, merchandise, and mail traveling on both the Mojave Road and on the Salt Lake Road.

No. 977: THE ARROWHEAD. The Arrowhead landmark can be seen for miles around. It is located in the San Bernardino Mountains. A marker is located in Wildwood Park, San Bernardino.

No. 985: DESERT TRAINING CENTER, CALIFORNIA-ARIZONA MANEUVER AREA ESTABLISHED BY GENERAL GEORGE S. PATTON, Jr.-CAMP IRON MOUNTAIN. This was one of 11 such camps built in the California-Arizona Desert to train troops during World War II. A plaque is E. of Needles on Highway 40.

No. 994: A.K. SMILEY PUBLIC LIBRARY. A.k. Smiley was a leader of the city's library movement. He donated this building and park to the citizens of Redlands in 1898. Marker is at 125 West Vine St., Redlands.

No. 1019: KIMBERLY CREST. Kimberly Crest was constructed in 1897. It was a Chateauesque-style carriage house. A marker is at 1325 Prospect Dr., Redlands.

No. 1028: MADONNA OF THE TRAIL. This is one of 12 identical statues placed in twelve states by the National Society of Daughters of the American Revolution. Marker is at 1100 Block, North Euclid Ave. Upland.

San Diego County

No. 49: ADOBE CHAPEL OF THE IMMACULATE CONCEPTION. It was built as the home of John Brown in 1850. It was converted to a church by Don Jose Aguirre in 1858. A marker is located at 3950 Conde St., Old Town, San Diego.

No. 50: BALLAST POINT WHALING STATION SITE. In 1857, three Johnson brothers and the twin Packard brothers surveyed this site for possibilities for a station to extract oil. The U.S. Government acquired the property in 1873 for Fort Rosecrans. A marker is at the base of Ballast Point, U.S. Naval Submarine Base, San Diego.

No. 51: OLD POINT LOMA LIGHTHOUSE. This lighthouse, built in 1854, was one of the first eight lighthouses on the Pacific Coast. A marker is located at Cabrillo National Monument, Point Loma, San Diego.

No. 52: MISSION DAM AND FLUME. After many attempts to supply water for crops and livestock at Mission San Diego de Alcala, a dam and flume system was finished between 1813-1816. A marker is in the parking lot of Fr. Junipero Serra Trail, San Diego.

No. 53: CASA DE ESTUDILLO. Three generations of the Don Jose Maria Estudillo's family made their home in Casa de Estudillo. A marker is at the corner of San Diego Ave. and Mason St., Old Town, San Diego.

No. 54: FORT STOCKTON. It was fortified by Carlos Carrillo in 1828. American forces took the town briefly in 1846. It was retaken by the Californios, and fell once more to the Americans. A marker is at the top of the hill west of Presidio Dr. in Presidio Park, Old Town, San Diego.

No. 55: FORT ROSECRANS NATIONAL CEMETERY. It was a burial ground before 1847. The graveyard became an army post cemetery in the 1860s. A marker is at Cabrillo Memorial Dr., Point Loma, San Diego.

No. 56: CABRILLO LANDING SITE. Juan Rodriguez Cabrillo **was** seeking the mythical site of the Strait of Anian (Northwest Passage) for Spain, on September 28, 1542. He brought three ships to Ballast Point. A marker is at U.S. Naval Submarine Base, San Diego.

No. 57: LA PUNTA DE LOS MUERTOS. Sailors and marines were buried here in 1782. A marker is at Market and Pacific Highway (State Highway 163) San Diego.

No. 59: SAN DIEGO PRESIDIO SITE. Soldiers, sailors, Indians, and Franciscan missionaries from New Spain occupied the land at Presidio Hill on May 17, 1769. Two months later, Fr. Junipero Serra established the first San Diego Mission on Presidio Hill. A marker is at the Serra Museum, Presidio Park, San Diego.

No. 60: CASA DE LOPEZ. It was built about 1835 by Juan Francisco Lopez. The Casa Largo, or Long House, was among the first substantial houses built in the Pueblo of San Diego. A marker is located at 3890 Twiggs St., Old Town, San Diego.

No. 61: OLD LA PLAYA. From 1770 to 1870, this was San Diego's port. Americans unofficially raised a U.S. flag there in 1829. A marker is on the left side of Rosecrans, Point Loma, San Diego.

No. 62: FORT ROSECRANS. President Millard Fillmore's executive order created a U.S. Preserve on Point Loma. From 1870 to 1873, the coast artillery evicted whalers from the site. A marker is at the base of Ballast Point, at the end of Rosecrans St., San Diego.

No. 63: PLAZA, SAN DIEGO VIEJO (WASHINGTON SQUARE). The plaza was at the center of the Mexican Pueblo of San Diego. A marker is at Old Town Plaza, San Diego State Historic Park.

No. 64: OLD LANDING, SITE OF EL DESEMBARCADEREO. The site was recognized as the landing place for small boats carrying freight and passengers to Old San Diego. A marker is on U.S. Naval Submarine Base, San Diego.

No. 65: THE WHALEY HOUSE. The San Diego County Court met here for 20 years. It was the first brick house built in San Diego. The bricks were made at Thomas Whaley's own kiln in Old Town in 1856. A marker is at 2734 Calhoun St., Old Town San Diego State Park.

No. 66: CONGRESS HALL SITE. This building was originally a two-story public house built by George Dewitt Clinton Washington Robinson about 1867. One of the last survivors of the Pony Express rode north from here. A marker is at 2734 Calhoun Str., Old Town, San Diego.

No.67: SERRA PALM SITE. This is the site where Padre Junipero Serra planted a palm when he arrived in San Diego. This is where four divisions of the Portola Expedition met July 1, 1769. A marker is in Presidio Park, San Diego.

No. 68: EL CAMPO SANTO. Between 1849 and 1897, there were 477 people buried on these grounds. A marker is on San Diego Ave., San Diego. (The plaque is currently in storage).

No.69: SITE OF FORT GUIJARROS. This is an outpost of Spain's far-flung empire. The fort was completed before 1800. Its major action came in the "Battle of San Diego Bay" with the American Brig Lelia Byrd, which was smuggling pelts. A marker is at the U.S. Naval Submarine Base, San Diego.

No. 70: CASA DE PEDRORENA. This was the home of Miguel de Pedrorena, who arrived in San Diego Viejo in 1838. He was a member of the Constitutional Convention in Monterey in 1849. A marker is at 2616 San Diego Ave., Old Town.

No. 71: CASA DE MACHADO. This adobe house was constructed in 1832 by Jose Manuel Machado, pioneer leather-jacket soldier of the Spanish Army. A marker is in Old Town, San Diego.

No. 72: CASA DE BANDINI. This house was built in 1827 by Jose and Juan Bandini for headquarters of Commodore Robert F. Stockton. It is the place where Kit Carson and Edward Beale delivered their urgent message of December 9, 1846, calling for reinforcements to be rushed to the aid of General Kearny. A marker exists at Mason and Calhoun Sts., Old Town, San Diego.

No. 73: CASA DE STEWART. This house was built by Jose Manuel Machado for his daughter, who was the wife of John C. Stewart. He was a shipmate of Richard Henry Dana. A marker is at Congress and Mason Sts., Old Town, San Diego.

No. 74: CASA DE CARRILLO. Presidio Comandante Francisco Maria Ruiz built this house next to his 1808 pear garden lake in 1821. He built it for his close friend and fellow soldier, Joaquin Carrillo. A marker is on Wallace St., Presidio Golf Course, San Diego.

No. 75: SITE OF CASA DE COTA. This adobe was built about 1835 by Father Lasuen, then president of the California missions. A marker is on State Highway 76 at 'Rancho Del Oro Dr., Oceanside.

No. 239: MISSION SAN LUIS REY DE FRANCIA. It is noted for its impressive architecture which is a composite of Spanish, Moorish and Mexican. A marker is on State Highway 76 at Rancho Del Oro, Oceanside.

No. 242: MISSION SAN DIEGO DE ALCALA. This was California's first mission. It was relocated from Presidio Hill to this site. A marker is 10818 San Diego Mission Rd., San Diego.

No. 243: ASISTENCIA SAN ANTONIO DE PALA. It's notable for its bell tower, or campanile. The chapel was built in 1816. A plaque is located on State Highway 76, Pala.

No. 244: DERBY DIKE. Until 1853, the San Diego River dumped tons of debris into the harbor. At times, it threatened to destroy Old Town San Diego. U.S. Topographical Corps built a dike that divered the waters into False Bay. A marker is in Presidio Park.

No. 304: VALLECITO STAGE DEPOT. It was built in 1852 at the edge of the Great Colorado Desert. It served the San Diego-San Antonio (Jackass) mail line. A marker is at Vallecito Stage Station County Park, Agua Caliente Springs.

No. 311: WARNER'S RANCH. Governor Micheltorena granted 44,322 acres to Juan Jose Warner, who built this house. The first Butterfield Stage stopped here. A marker is on County Highway 52 at Junction of State Highway 79. Warner Springs.

No. 369: CHAPEL OF SANTA YSABEL. This was a mission outpost with about 450 neophytes. A marker is on State Highway 79, Santa Ysabel.

No. 411: CAMP STONE STORE. The pioneer Gaskill brothers built this store in 1868. It was raided by border bandits on December 4, 1875. A marker is located Camp Cr., Campo.

No. 412: JULIAN. Ex-confederate soldier Drury D. Batley laid out the town on his farmland. He named it for his cousin Michael S. Julian. A private plaque is in Julian Memorial Park.

No. 425: LA CANADA DE LOS COCHES RANCHO. It commemorates Canada de Los Coches Rancho. A marker is located at 13468 Old Highway 80, Lakeside.

No. 452: MULE HILL. The battle of San Pasquel was fought near here. General Stephen Kearny's command was again attacked by Californios. The Americans counter-attacked and occupied this hill. Short of food, they ate mule meat and named the place Mule Hill. A marker is on Pomerado Rd., Escondido.

No. 472: BOX CANYON. The old road, known as the Sonora, Colorado River, or Southern Emigrant Trail, traversed Box Canyon. The Mormon Battalion, using hand tools, hewed a passage through the rocky walls of the narrow gorge and opened the first road into Southern California. Marker is on County Road 52, Anza-Borrego Desert State Park.

No. 482: CAMP WRIGHT. This site was named for Brigadier General George Wright, who commanded the Pacific Department and California District. A marker is located on State Highway 79., Oak Grove.

No. 491: OAK GROVE STAGE STATION. This is one of the few remaining stations on the Butterfield Overland Mail Route. A marker is on State Highway 79, Oak Grove.

No. 523: SAN DIEGO BARRACKS. New San Diego was established as a quartermaster depot in 1850 to supply military establishes in Southern California. A marker is located on Market St., San Diego.

No. 533: SAN PASQUAL BATTLEFIELD STATE HISTORIC PARK. A detachment of U.S. Dragoons was met on this site by native California lancers under General Andres Pico. In the battle, severe losses were suffered by the Americans. General Kearney rallied his men and the Californios withdrew. A marker is located at San Pasqual Battlefield State Historic Park.

No. 538: FIRST PUBLICALLY OWNED SCHOOL BUILDING. The Mason St. School, District No. 1, was erected on this site in 1865. San Diego County covered an area larger than three New England states. A marker is at 3966 Mason St., Old Town San Diego State Park.

No. 562: LA CHRISTIANITA. Near this spring, the first Christian baptism in Alta California was performed. A plaque is in the San Clemente Civic Center, San Clemente.

No. 616: LAS FLORES ASISTENCIA. This tile-roofed adobe chapel and hostel at Los Flores served as the asistencia to Mission San Luis Rey. It was the site of the April 1838 battle between Juan Bautista Alvarado and Carlos Antonio Carillo who were contesting the provincial governorship of Alta California.

No. 626: BANCROFT RANCH HOUSE. This adobe was built in 1863 by A.S. Ellsworth as the home for Captain Rufus K. Porter and family. It's curved timbers were brought from the Clarissa Andrews, a famed coaling hulk formerly of the Pacific Mail Steamship Co. A marker is at Memory and Bancroft Dr., Spring Valley.

No. 634: EL VADO: This route was opened by Captain Juan Bautista de Anza and Father Garces in 1774. Anza's expedition camped near El Vado (The Ford). A marker is at Anza-Borrego Springs Park.

No. 635: LOS PUERTECITOS. Juan Bautista's expedition marched through here on its way to San Francisco. Marker is on State Highway 78, Ocotillo Wells.

No. 639: PALM SPRINGS. Mexican pioneers coming to California in 1862 rested here. The site was also a Butterfield Stage Station stop. A marker is on Vallecito Creek Road, Anza Borrego Desert State Park.

No. 647: BUTTEREFIELD OVERLAND MAIL ROUTE. This pass was used by the Mormon Battalion, Kearney's Army of the West, to reach the cooler valleys to the north. A marker is located in the Anza-Borrego Desert State Park.

No. 673: SAN GREGORIO. Somewhere in this narrow valley, the Anza Expedition made their camps in 1774 and 1775. The men dug a series of wells deeper than the height of a man to find water for the 240 people and for the livestock. Ask at park visitor center for the marker.

No. 711: MONTGOMERY MEMORIAL. At Otay Mesa, in 1883, John Joseph Montgomery made the first flight in a heavier than air craft 20 years before the Wright Brothers. The marker is at Coronado Ave. and Beyer Blvd., South San Diego.

No. 750: PEG LEG SMITH MONUMENT. Thomas L. Smith, better known as Peg Leg, found gold in the Anza-Borrego Desert, and then couldn't find the site again. In recent years, the site was rediscovered and the easy gold pickings removed. A marker is at Garnet Ave. and Pico St., Anza-Borrego Desert State Park.

No. 764: SITE OF KATE O. SESSIONS NURSERY. This plaque commemorates the life and influence of a woman who envisioned a beautiful San Diego. She operated a nursery and gained world renown as a horticulturist. Marker is at Garnet Ave. and Pico St., San Diego.

No. 784: EL CAMINO REAL. This plaque was placed on the 250th anniversary of the birth of California's apostle, Padre Junipero Serra. A marker is at 10818 San Diego Mission Road, San Diego.

No. 785: SANTA CATARINA. The water spring was named by Captain Juan Bautista when his exploration party camped here in March 14, 1774. Ask for the Santa Catarina Springs marker at the visitor center.

No. 793: SAN FELIPE VALLEY AND STAGE STATION. Explorers, trappers, soldiers and emigrants crossed these ancient trade routes of Kamia, Cahuilla, Diegueno and Luiseno Indians. A marker is on County Highway S2, near Anza-Borrego Desert State Park.

No.798: SAN DIEGO STATE COLLEGE, SITE OF FIRST DOCTORATE DEGREE GRANTED BY THE CALIFORNIA STATE COLLEGE SYSTEM. San Diego State College was the first of the California State Colleges to grant a doctorate degree when it conferred an honorary doctorate on the late President of the United States, John F. Kennedy. A marker is at the entrance to the service area of Cox Arenam, San Diego.

No. 818: FIRST MILITARY FLYING SCHOOL IN AMERICA. Glenn Curtiss founded the first military flying school in America on January 17, 1911. A marker is located at the entrance to Gate 5, Naval Air Station, North Island, Coronado.

No. 830: OLD TOWN SAN DIEGO STATE HISTORIC PARK. Old Town was settled by pensioned soldiers from the presidio. The Stars and Stripes was raised over the plaza in 1846. A plaque is located on the west side of the plaza at 4016 Wallace St., San Diego.

No. 844: HOTEL DEL CORONADO. This Victorian hotel was built in 1887. It is one of America's largest wooden buildings. A plaque is located in the Hotel Garden Patio, 1500 Orange Ave., Coronado.

No. 858: THE PEDRO FAGES TRAIL. Colonel Pedro Fages was headed east after army deserters when he made the first entry into Oriflamme Canyon. A marker is 8 miles east of Julian.

No. 891: SPANISH LANDING. Near this point, sea and land parties of the Portola Expedition met in 1769. The scurvy-weakened survivors of the voyage established a camp. Together, they began the Spanish occupation of Alta California. A marker is at Spanish Landing Park, Harbor Dr. San Diego.

No. 940: RANCHO GUAJOME. It was formerly attached to Mission San Luis Rey. This 2,219-acre ranch was briefly owned by two mission Indians. A marker exists at Rancho Guajome Regional Park, Vista.

No. 982: HISTORIC PLANNED COMMUNITY OF RANCHO SANTA FE. Rancho Santa Fe began as Rancho San Dieguito, a land grant of 9,000 acres. The Santa Fe Railroad Company later used the property plant thousands of eucalyptus trees for use as railroad ties. A marker is on Village Green, Rancho Santa Fe.

No. 1020: LEO CARRILLO RANCH (RANCHO DE LOS KIOTES) Leo Carrillo built the adobe and wood buildings in 1937 and 1940. They were built as a retreat, working ranch, and a tribute to old California culture. A marker is in front of the Inn, Rancho Santa Fe.

No. 1026: SANTA MARGARITA RANCH HOUSE. It was named by the Portola Expedition in July 1769 for St. Margaret of Antioch. A marker is at the U.S. Marine Corp Camp Pendleton.

No. 1030: STAR OF INDIA. The Star of India is a three-masted bark. It is the oldest iron-hulled merchant ship afloat. It is docked at 1306 North Harbor Dr., San Diego.

No. 1031: FERYBOAT BERKELEY. These steam ferryboat was the first successful West Coast built and operated ferry to be driven by a screw propeller as opposed to side-wheels. It's docked at 1306 North Harbor Drive, San Diego.

No. 1044: GIANT DIPPER ROLLER COASTER. The 1925 Giant Dipper Roller Coaster is a large wooden scaffolded roller coaster. Its highest hill reaches 75 feet. It is one of two wooden roller coasters to remain on the West Coast.

San Francisco County

No. 79: PRESIDIO OF SAN FRANCISCO. Established on September 17, 1776, the San Francisco Presidio has been used as a military headquarters by Spain, Mexico and the United States. A marker is at Funston Ave. and Lincoln Blvd., San Francisco.

No. 80: MONTGOMERY BLOCK. This is the site of San Francisco's first fireproof building. It was built in 1853 by Henry Wager Halleck. This building escaped destruction in the earthquake and fire of 1906. A marker is at 600 Montgomery Street, San Francisco.

No. 81: LANDING PLACE OF CAPTAIN J.B. MONTGOMERY. When the water came up to Montgomery Street, Commander John. B. Montgomery brought his sloop near this spot to raise the Stars and Stripes on the plaza. A marker is located at 552 Montgomery St., San Francisco.

No. 82: CASTILLO DE SAN JOAQUIN. The first ship to enter San Francisco Bay was the San Carlos. It dropped anchor off this point August 5, 1775. A marker is at the corner of Fort Wall, San Francisco. (It's below Golden Gate Bridge).

No. 83: SHORELINE MARKERS. This tablet marks the shoreline of San Francisco Bay at the time of the discovery of gold in California. A plaque is in the sidewalk, Bush and Market Sts. San Francisco.

No. 84: RINCON HILL. This was the home of William Tecumseh Sherman, William C. Ralston, William Gwin, H.H. Bancroft and others. A plaque is mounted on the retaining wall of St. Mary's Hospital.

No. 85: OFFICE OF THE CALIFORNIA STAR NEWSPAPER. This was the first newspaper in San Francisco. It was published by Sam Brannan with Elbert P. Jones as editor. A marker is at Washington St. and Brenham Place, San Francisco.

No. 86: CALIFORNIA THEATRE. On January 18, 1869, The California Theatre opened with a broad cast of actors and actresses. A marker can be found at 430 Bush St., San Francisco.

No. 87: SITE OF FIRST U.S. BRANCH MINT IN CALIFORNIA. The first United States branch mint in San Francisco was authorized by Congress July 3, 1852. A marker is located at 608-610 Commercial St., San Francisco.

No. 88: NIANTIC HOTEL. The emigrant ship *Niantic* stood here when the water came up to Montgomery St. The ship was converted to other uses. It was covered with a shingle roof with offices and stores on the deck. A marker is in the lower level of Two Transamerica Center, San Francisco.

No. 89: SITE OF PARROTT GRANITE BLOCK. The three-story building, built by Chinese labor, was of granite blocks brought from China. The 1906 earthquake and fire did little damage to the building. A marker is at California and Montgomery, San Francisco.

No. 90: FORT GUNNYBAGS. This is the site of the headquarters of the Vigilance Committee of 1856. On June 21, 1856, Judge David S. Terry was arrested and confined in a cell. The Vigilance Committee, fearing that his friends might attempt to rescue him, decided to fortify the building with gunnysacks filled with sand. A marker is at Davis and Front Sts., San Francisco.

No. 91: TELEGRAPH HILL. A signal station was erected on Telegraph Hill in 1849 from which to observe the incoming vessels. A tall pole with movable arms was used to signal people in the town below whether sailing vessels or the sidewheel vessels of the Pacific mail were passing through the Golden Gate. In September 1853, the first telegraph in California, which extended eight miles to Point Lobos, was stationed here, giving the hill its name. A plaque is in the lobby of the Coit Tower.

No. 119: PORTSMOUTH PLAZA. This plaza was named for the USS Portsmouth, commanded by Captain John B. Montgomery. Montgomery Street was named for him. A plaque can be seen in Portsmouth Square Park between Kearny and Washington St.

No. 192: EL DORADO, PARKER HOUSE, AND DENNISON'S EXCHANGE. The El Dorado, the Parker House, and Dennison's Exchange were among the most famous hotel and gambling resorts around San Francisco in the early 1980s. The Jenny Lind Theatre replaced the Parker House in 1850. A marker is at 750 Kearny St., San Francisco.

No. 236: ENTRANCE OF THE SAN CARLOS INTO SAN FRANCISCO BAY. The Spanish Packet, *San Carlos* became the first ship to enter San Francisco Bay. A Marker is at Beach and Larkin Streets, San Francisco.

No. 327-1 SITE OF ORIGINAL MISSION DELORES CHAPEL AND DOLORES LAGOON. On June 29, 1776, Father Francisco Palou, a member of the De Anza expedition, had a brushwood shelter built on the edge of a now-vanished lake. Here he offered the first mass. A marker is at Camp and Albion Sts., San Francisco.

No. 328: LONG WHARF. The old Central or Long Wharf was built from the bank in the middle of the block between Sacramento and Clay Streets. It reached 800-feet into the Bay. After 1950, it was extended 2,000 feet and the Pacific mail steamers and other large vessels anchored there. Central or Long Wharf is now Commercial Street. A marker is at Leidsdorff and Commercial Sts., San Francisco.

No. 408: SITE OF THE FIRST MEETING OF FREMASONS HELD IN CALIFORNIA. On November 9, 1849, a charter was granted by the Grand Lodge of The District of Columbia for th eorganzation of California Lodge 13. It is now California Lodge 1. A plaque is at 728 Montgomery St. San Francisco.

No. 453: LUCAS, TURNER & CO. BANK (SHERMAN'S BANK). William Tecumseh Sherman established the branch bank of Lucas, Turner and Co. in San Francisco in 1853. He successfully carried the bank through the financial crisis of 1855. A marker is at Montgomery and Jackson, San Francisco.

No. 454: WOODWARD'S GARDENS. R. B. Woodward opened his gardens to the public in 1866. It was an amusement park catering to all tastes. It was San Francisco's most popular resort until it closed in 1892. A marker is on the corner of Mission and Duboce Sts., San Francisco.

No. 459: SITE OF THE BRICK BUILDING OF THE FIRM OF MELLUS AND HOWARD. The Mellus and Howard Warehouse, erected in 1848, was the home of California Pioneers, the oldest historical society in the state. A marker is at 555 Montgomery Street, San Francisco.

No. 462: SITE OF FIRST JEWISH RELIGIOUS SERVICES IN SAN FRANCISCO. Forty pioneers of the Jewish faith gathered on September 26, 1849, Yom Kippur (5610), and participated in the first Jewish religious services in San Francisco. A marker is at 735 Montgomery, San Francisco.

No. 500: EASTERN TERMINUS OF CLAY STRET HILL RAILROAD. The Clay Street Hill Railroad Company was the first cable railroad system in the world. It was invented and installed by Andrew S. Hallidie. It started operation on August 1, 1873. A marker is located at Portsmouth Plaza, Clay and Brenham Sts., San Francisco.

No. 587: FIRST PUBLIC SCHOOL. The first public school in California was located here. It opened on April 3, 1848 on the southwest corner of Portsmouth Square. A marker is located in Portsmouth Plaza, Clay and Brenham Sts., San Francisco.

No. 623: UNION SQUARE. This was the center of San Francisco in pioneer days. It was deeded for public use January 3, 1850 by John White Geary. A marker is at Geary and Powell Sts., San Francisco.

No. 650: SITE OF THE WHAT CHEER HOUSE. The famous "What Cheer House" was a unique hotel opened in 1852 by R.B. Woodward. It was destroyed by fire in 1906. The What Cheer House catered to men only. It permitted no liquor on the premises, and housed San Francisco's first free library and first museum. See the marker at Sacramento and Leidesdorff Sts., San Francisco.

No. 691. SARCOPHAGUS OF THOMAS STARR KING. Thomas Starr King was described as an apostle of liberty, humanitarian, and a Unitarian minister. During the Civil War, he bound California to the Union and led her to excel all other states in support of the United States Sanitary Commission. A marker is at First Unitarian Church, Franklin between Starr King and Geary, San Francisco.

No. 754: SITE OF THE MARK HOPKINS INSTITUTE OF THE ARTS. On February 1893, Edward F. Searles donated the Hopkins Mansion to the University of California in trust for the San Francisco Art Institute. A marker is at California and Mason, San Francisco.

No. 760: SITE OF LAUREL HILL CEMETERY. Many of the famous builders of the west, as well as civic and military leaders are buried here. A marker is at 3333 California Street, San Francisco.

No. 772: ORIGINAL SITE OF ST. MARY'S COLLEGE. In August, 1863, St. Mary's College opened with a faculty of two diocesan priests, four laymen, and two student teachers. A marker is at the intersection of Mission and College Sts., San Francisco.

No. 784: EL CAMINO REAL. A plaque was placed on the 250th anniversary of the birth of California's apostle, Padre Junipero Serra. A marker is located at Mission San Diego de Alcala.

No. 791: ORIGINAL SITE OF THE BANCROFT LIBRARY. Hubert Howe Bancroft began collecting a wealth of material which resulted in the writing of his monumental history of western North America. A marker is at 1538 Valencia St., San Francisco.

No. 810: SITE OF OLD ST. MARY'S CHURCH. Once the city's most prominent buildings, it is built of brick brought around the Horn in sailing ships. A marker is located at California and Grant Ave., San Francisco.

No. 819: HUDSON'S BAY COMPANY HEADQUARTERS. The chief trader was William G. Tae. He purchased the property and started operations in 1841. Marker is at 505 Montgomery.

No. 841: THE CONSERVATORY. California's first municipal green house was completed in 1879. It is patterned after the Kew Gardens, England. A marker is in Golden Gate Park.

No. 861: SITE OF THE FIRST CALIFORNIA STATE FAIR. California's first state fair was held in San Francisco on October 4, 1854. It was sponsored the California State Agricultural Society. The exhibition of horses, cattle, mules and other stock, as well as agricultural machinery promoted the state's agricultural industry. A different city held the fair each year until Sacramento became the permanent location in 1861. Marker is at 269 Bush St.

No. 875: OLD UNITED STATES MINT. It was San Francisco's second mint (1869). It served as a clearing-house bank, thus aiding in the city's reconstruction.

No. 876: CITY OF PARIS BUILDING. In 1850, the Verdier brothers opened a store aboard the ship La Ville de Paris. In 1896, it moved into a building. The building was damaged by the 1906 earthquake. A marker is on corner of Geary and Stockton Sts., San Francisco.

No. 937: SITE OF INVENTION OF THE THREE-REEL SLOT MACHINE. Charles Augustus Fey invented the first coin-operated three-reel slot machine in San Francisco in 1895. He manufactured the "Liberty Bell" gaming devices in his workshop at 406 Market Street.

No. 941: FARNSWORTH'S GREEN STREET LAB. In a simple laboratory at 202 Green Street Philo Taylor Farnsworth invented and patented the first operational all-electronic television system. The 21-year old and several dedicated assistants transmitted on September 7, 1927, the first all-electronic image. A marker is at Sansome and Green Sts., San Francisco.

No. 964: BIRTHPLACE OF THE UNITED NATIONS, WAR MEMORIAL COMPLEX. Fifty nations participated in the drafting of the United Nations Charter which was unanimously adopted June 25, 1945. A marker is at Civic Center, in the 400 block of Van Ness, San Francisco.

No. 974: GOLDEN GATE BRIDGE. The 4,200-foot bridge was the longest in the world until 1959. Dedication marker is in the observation area, north end of the bridge.

No. 1002: SITE OF FIRST DYNAMITE FACTORY IN THE UNITED STATES. The nation's first dynamite was made in what is now Glen Canyon Park in 1868. The factory did not last long. An explosion destroyed the facility. A marker located in Glen Canyon Park, San Francisco.

No. 1010: ORIGINAL SITE OF THE THIRD BAPTIST CHURCH (FORMERLY THE FIRST COLORED BAPTIST CHURCH). The church was organized in the home of William Davis. The congregation purchased the old First Baptist Church and moved it to 1399 McAllister St. A marker is at Grant Ave. and Greenwich, San Francisco.

No. 1024: JUANA BRIONES, PIONEER SETTLER OF YERBA BUENA. Juana Briones was born in Hispanic California. She transformed an isolated cove in the Mexican hamlet of Yerba Buena into her rancho. A marker is at Washington Square Park, San Francisco.

San Joaquin County

No. 149: BENSON'S FERRY. This river ferry was started in 1849. John Benson purchased it in 1852. Benson laid out the principal wagon road between Sacramento and Stockton. Benson was murdered in 1859 and the ferry was run by his son-in-law, Ed Gayetty. There's a marker on the North Fork of the Mokelumne River.

No. 155: LONE STAR MILL. A sawmill built in 1852 on the Mokelumne River was moved to Hodge and Terry's ranch in 1854. A flour mill was attached the following year. When the mill burned, it was rebuilt on the same site as the Lone Star Mill. A marker is at the entrance to Stillman L. Magee Park, north of Clements.

No. 162: SITE OF MOKELUMNE CITY. The town was established in 1850. It was the second largest town in the county. The flood of 1862 destroyed the town. A marker is located at Cameron Road and Thornton Road.

No. 163: SITE OF WOOD'S FERRY AND WOOD'S BRIDGE. In 1852, immediately after he arrived and completed his cabin, Jeremiah H. Woods proceeded to build a ferryboat. He established a crossing known as Wood's Ferry. In 1858, he built a toll bridge at the old ferry crossing. He charged $1 for a pair of animals and wagon, and 50 cents for every additional pair of animals and wagon. A marker is at County Highway J10, Woodbridge.

No. 165: WEBER POINT. Charles M. Weber built a two-story adobe and redwood home in 1850. Weber was the founder of Stockton. It was one of the first elaborate residences in Stockton. A marker is on Center St. between Channel and Miner Sts., Stockton.

No 178: SITE OF FIRST BUILDING IN PRESENT CITY OF STOCKTON. The first settlers arrived at Rancho del Campo de los Frances. Thomas Lindsay built the first dwelling, a tule hut on this site. A marker is at City Hall, between Miner and El Dorado Sts., Stockton.

No. 214: SITE OF BATTLE BETWEEN FORCES UNDER GENERAL VALLEJO AND SAN JOAQUIN VALLEY INDIAN. In 1829, the Governor-General of California directed General Mariano Vallejo to punish the Cosumnes Indians for their raids on local ranches. The battle is one of he few fought in California in which cannons were actually used. A marker is at the confluence of the San Joaquin and Stanislaus Rivers.

No. 358: TOWN OF WOODBRIDGE. In 1852, Jeremiah H. Woods and Alexander McQueen established a ferry across the Mokelumne River. In 1858, Woods built a bridge at the site of the ferry. Marker is on County Highway J10, Woodbridge.

No. 365: LOCKEFORD (LOCKE'S FORD) Dr. Dean Jewett Locke and his brother Elmer H. Locke built the first cabin on this section in 1851. Disturbed by grizzly bears, they spent their nights in the oak trees. Dr. Locke built and maintained a ford across the Mokelumne River. His wife, Delia, named the town he laid out on his ranch, Lockeford.

No. 436: NEW HOPE. Twenty Mormon pioneer miners from the ship *Brooklyn* founded the first known agricultural colony in the San Joaquin Valley. They planted the first wheat and crops that they irrigated by the "pole and bucket" method. See the marker at Fourth and Locust, Ripon.

No. 437: FIRST LANDING PLACE OF SAILING LAUNCH COMET. The first known sail launch to ascend from San Francisco to landed here in New Hope in 1846. It carried 20 Mormon pioneers. A marker is located at the entrance to Mossdale Crossing and Ramp.

No. 513: BURIAL PLACE OF JOHN BROWN (JUAN FLACO). In 1846, during the American Conquest of California, John Brown, nicknamed Juan Flaco, rode from Los Angeles to San Francisco in four days to warn Commodore Stockton of the siege of Los Angeles. He was dubbed the "Paul Revere of California". Plaque is at 1100 Weber St., Stockton.

No. 520: SAN JOAQUIN VALLEY COLLEGE. The college was built through subscription by the residents of Woodbridge and dedicated as Woodbridge Seminary in 1879. Marker is at 18500 N. Lilac St., Woodbridge.

No. 668: FRENCH CAMP. This was the terminus of the Oregon-California Trail. Marker is on Elm St. at French Camp.

No. 740: CARNEGIE. It had a population of 3,500, with a post office, a company store, hotels, saloons, a bandstand and hundreds of homes. The Carnegie Brick and Pottery Company had 45 kilns and 13 tall smokestacks. A marker is located at the Carnegie State Vehecular Recreation Area.

No. 755: CORRAL HOLLOW. Through here passed the 49ers and the first mail to the Tuolumne mines. Men and animals received food and drink at Wright's Zink House. A marker is on Corral Hollow Road, Tracy.

No. 765: TEMPLE ISRAEL CEMETERY. The land was donated by Charles M. Weber in 1851 for use as a cemetery by the Jewish Community of Stockton. A marker is on E. Acacia, Stockton.

No. 777: SITE OF SAN JOAQUIN CITY. This river town was established in 1849. The town played an important part in west side grain farming and cattle raising. Marker is on County Hwy J3, Tracy.

No. 780-7: FIRST TRANSCONTINENTAL RAILROAD-SITE OF COMPLETION OF PACIFIC RAILROAD. Construction of the San Joaquin River bridge completed the last link of the transcontinental railroad. A marker is located at I-5 and I-205, Tracy.

No. 801: REUEL COLT GRIDLEY MONUMENT. This monument was erected in honor of his friend by Rawlins Post. Both men served in the Grand Army of the Republic. A marker is at Stockton Rural Cemetery.

No. 931: LODI ARCH. The arch was designed by architect E.B. Brown and built in 1907 for the Lodi Tokay Carnival. The arch has been unaltered since construction. A marker is at E. Pine and Sacramento Sts., Lodi.

No. 934: TEMPORARY DETENTION CAMPS FOR JAPANESE AMERICANS-STOCKTON ASSEMBLY CENTER. People of Japanese origin were confined to the San Joaquin County Fairgrounds during World War II. A marker is located at the fairgrounds, Airport Way, Stockton.

No. 935: CALIFORNIA CHICORY WORKS. This was the largest chicory supplier in America while operating in the 1890s. Chicory roots were roasted, ground and used as a coffee additive. A marker is at 1672 W. Bowman, French Camp.

No, 995 TRAIL OF THE JOHN C. FREMONT 1844 EXPEDITION. Fremont's second expedition overland in 1843-44 was the first in which he reached California. A marker is junction of Hwy 88 and Calaveras River.

No. 1016: STOCKTON DEVELOPMENT CENTER. The Stockton Development Center opened in 1853 as the Insane Asylum of California at Stockton. California's legislature was convinced that turbulence of the gold rush had caused many o suffer mental problems. A marker is at 510 E. Magnolia, Stockton.

No. 1039: SIKH TEMPLE SITE. The Sikhs are from the Punjab region of India. Most were drawn to agriculture in the Sacramento and San Joaquin valleys. Stockton's Sikh Temple is an important Sikh institution. A marker is at 1930 S. Grant Street, Stockton.

San Luis Obispo County

No. 325: MISSION SAN LUIS OBISPO DE TOLOSA. This was the fifth in the chain of 21 missions stretching from San Diego to Sonoma. A marker is on Monterey between Chorro and Broad Sts., San Luis Obispo.

No.326: MISSION SAN MIGUEL ARCANGEL. This site was selected because of the number of Salinan Indians that lived in the area. It was 16th in the chain of 21 missions. A marker is at the corner of Mission St. and San Luis Obispo Rd., San Miguel.

No. 364: SANTA MARGARITA ASISTENCIA. This was an outpost or chapel and storehouse for Mission San Luis Obispo. The mission padres and the Indians carried on extensive grain cultivation. A marker is at Yerba Buena Ave. and F St., Santa Margarita.

No. 542: ESTRELLA ADOBE CHURCH. This was the first Protestant church in the northern part of San Luis Obispo County. A marker is on Airport Rd., Paso Robles.

No. 640: HEARST SAN SIMEON STATE HISTORICAL PARK. Between 1919 and 1947 William Randolph Hearst created *La Cuesta Encantada* (The Enchanted Hill). The Hearst castle was given to the State of California in 1858 as a memorial to William Randolph Hearst. A marker is at entrance to rest area, Hearst San Simeon State Historical Monument.

No. 720: DALLIDET ADOBE. This was the home of Pierre Hyppolite Dallidet, a native of France. The property was donated to the state by his son, Paul Dallidet, in 1953. A marker is at 1309 Toro, San Luis Obispo.

No. 726: THE SEBASTIAN STORE. It was built in 1860s at Whaling Point. It was moved to its present location in 1878. A marker is at San Simeon Road, San Simeon.

No. 802: AH LOUIS STORE. This was the first Chinese store in the county. It sold goods to the Chinese coolies who dug the eight tunnels through the Mountains of Cuesta for the Southern Pacific Railroad. A marker is at 800 Palm St., San Luis Obispo.

No. 821: MORRO ROCK. It served as an important mariner's navigation landfall for more than three hundred years. Morro Reef was chronicled in the diaries of Portola. It's sometimes called the "*Gibraltar of the Pacific*". A marker is at the foot of Morro Rock.

No. 936: RIOS-CALEDONIA ADOBE. Petronilo Rios built this two-story adobe with Indian labor. It was his home and headquarters for his sheep and cattle operations. It also served as a hotel and stage stop. A marker is at 700 Mission St., San Miguel.

No. 939: TWENTIETH CENTURY FOLK ART ENVIRONMENTS. Nitt Witt Ridge is the creation of Harold Beal, a Cambria Pines pioneer. It is a revealing memorial to Art's unique cosmic humor and zest for life. A marker is at 881 Hillcrest Dr., Cambria Pines.

No. 958: ADMINISTRATION AND VETERAN'S MEMORIAL BUILDING. It was a private school for boys, a veteran's memorial building, and county offices. It is currently the seat of municipal government. A marker is at 6500 Palma Ave. Atascadero.

No. 1033: RANCHO NIPOMO. It is almost 38,000 acres in size. It was granted to Boston sea Captain William Goodwin Dana in 1837. It was long-known as a hospitable place for travelers. A marker is at 6715 Oakglen Ave., Nipomo.

San Mateo County

No. 2: PORTOLA JOURNEY'S END. In 1769, Portola's expedition of 63 men and 200 horses and mules, camped near El Palo Alto, *the tall tree*. They had traveled from San Diego in search of Monterey but instead found the Bay of San Francisco. A marker is at E Creek Dr. and Alma St., Menlo Park.

No. 19: BRODERICK-TERRY DUELING PLACE. On September 13, U.S. Senator David C. Broderick and Chief Justice David S. Terry of the California Supreme Court fought the famous duel that ended dueling in California. Senator Broderick was mortally wounded. A marker is at 1100 Lake Merced Blvd., Daly City.

No. 21: PORTOLA EXPEDITION CAMP. The Portola expedition camped close to the mouth of Pilarcitos Creek on October 28 and 29. Portola, himself, was very ill. A marker is at the Mouth of Pilarcitos Creek, Half Moon Bay.

No. 22: PORTOLA EXPEDITION CAMP. The Indian village on the north bank of Purisma Creek was named Las Pulgas by the army engineer because the Portola party became covered with fleas.

No. 23: PORTOLA EXPEDITION CAMP. The Portola expedition camped at Gazos Creek Rd.

No. 24: PORTOLA EXPEDITION CAMP. The Portola Expedition camped near San Pedro Creek, near an Indian village. Marker is at Crespi Dr. and Hwy 1.

No. 25: PORTOLA EXPEDITION CAMP. The expedition camped at the foot of Montara Mountain. Needing food badly, the explorers found a plentiful supply of mussels. They named the camp *El Rincon de las Almejas.*

No. 26: PORTOLA EXPEDITION CAMP. Portola and party camped on San Gregoria Creek. Tired and sick, the party rested here for two days.

No. 27: PORTOLA EXPEDITION PARTY. Portola and party camped near a lagoon now covered by San Andreas Lake on November 4. A plaque is 500 feet W. on Hillcrest Ave., Millbrae.

No. 47: ANZA EXPEDITION CAMP. B. de Anza camped after exploring the peninsula and selecting the sites for the Mission and Presidio of San Francisco. Marker is 300 feet West of San Mateo.

No. 48: ANZA EXPEDITION CAMP. Anza's party, on its way to locate sites for a presidio and mission of San Francisco, camped at a dry watercourse a short league beyond Arroyo de San Mateo. Marker is at El Camino and Ralston, Burlingame.

No. 93: WOODSIDE STORE. Built in 1854 among sawmills and redwood groves, Dr. R.O. Tripp operated a store. He was also a dentist, librarian, postmaster and community leader. A marker is on corner of Kings Mint. Rd. and Tripp Rd., Woodside.

No. 94: PORTOLA EXPEDITION CAMP. Portola and party camped at *Laguna Grande.* A marker is at Crystal Springs Dam, San Mateo.

No. 343: OLD STORE AT LA HONDA. In 1861, John Sears settled in the mountains 17 miles from Redwood City. He named the place La Honda and built a store there. A marker is on Highway 84.

No, 375: TUNITAS BEACH, INDIAN VILLAGE SITE ON PORTOLA ROUTE. Portola discovered an Indian village on Tunitas Creek. It was on *Rancho Canada de Verde y Arroyo de la Purisma.* Marker is at Tunitas Creek, Half Moon Bay.

No. 391: SANCHEZ ADOBE. This was the home of Francisco Sanchez, alcalde of San Francisco. A marker is at Sanchez Adobe County Park, Pacifica.

No. 393: THE HOSPICE (OUTPOST OF MISSION DELORES). Located here was a hospice built by Spanish padres on El Camino Real. A marker is on Baywood and El Camino Real.

394: SITE OF THE DISCOVERY OF SAN FRANCISCO BAY. While camped by the creek of this valley, scouting parties brought news of a body of water to the east. The party climbed to the summit of Sweeney Ridge an beheld the Bay of San Francisco for the first time. A marker is on Crespi Dr. and Hwy 1, Pacifica.

No. 474: SITE OF THE FORMER VILLAGE OF SEARSVILLE. John Sears arrived in 1854. The buildings in this community were removed in 1891 as water rose behind the new dam. Marker is at intersection of Sandhill and Portola Roads, Woodside.

No. 478: SITE OF SAN MATEO COUNTY'S FIRST SAW MILL. The mill was built by Charles Brown in 1847. At the same time, Dennis Martin was building a second mill on San Francisco Creek. These mills were similar to John Sutter's famous mill at Coloma. A marker is Woodside Road and Portola Road, Woodside.

No. 816: UNION CEMETERY. This cemetery was established before the first shots were fired at Fort Sumter that brought on the Civil War A marker exists at El Camino Real and Woodside Road, Redwood City.

No. 825: CASA DE TABLETA. This structure was built by Felix Buelna in the 1850s. It served as a gambling retreat and meeting place for Mexican Californios. A marker is at 3915 Alpine Road, Portola Valley.

No. 846: BURLINGAME RAILROAD STATION. This was the first permanent building in the Mission Revival style of architecture. The roof used 18th century tiles from the Mission San Antonio de Padua at Jolon and the Mission Dolores Asistencia at San Mateo. A marker is at 290 California Dr., Burlingame.

No. 856: RALSTON HALL. This redwood structure was built in 1868 by William Chapman Ralston. A marker is at Campus of College of Notre Dame, 1500 Ralston Ave., Belmont.

No. 886: CAROLANDS. Harriet Pullman Carolan was heiress to the Pullman railroad car company fortune. She built this lavis mini-palace in 1915-16. A marker is located at 565 Remillard Rd., Hillsborough.

No. 906: STEELE BROTHERS DAIRY RANCHES. Steele Brothers was one of the first large-scale commercial cheese and dairy businesses in the state. A marker is at Ano Nuevo State Reserve, Pescadero.

No. 907: FILOLI. This is described as one of the most outstanding grand estates of the late 1800s. A marker is at Filoli Center, Canada Rd., Woodside.

No. 909: OUR LADY OF THE WAYSIDE. This country church was built in 1912. It was the first design of architect Timothy L. Pflueger. It shows his awareness of the Spanish California missions. A marker is at 930 Portola Rd., Portola Valley.

No. 930: PIGEON POINT LIGHTHOUSE. This brick lighthouse was built to incorporate a French first order Fresnel lens. Although no longer used, the lens is still operable. Marker is at intersection of Pigeon Point Rd. and State Hwy 1.

No. 934: TEMPORARY DETENTION CAMPS FOR JAPANESE AMERICANS-TANFORAN ASSEMBLY CENTER. People of Japanese ancestry were held in these detention centers during World War II. A marker is located at Tanforan Park Shopping Center.

No. 939: TWENTIETH CENTURY FOLK ART ENVIRONMENTS. The late John Guidici, a retired gardener, began landscaping his Menlo Park house in 1932. He used cement local sand, and the shells he found at local beaches. A marker is at 262 Princeton Road, Menlo Park.

No. 949: FIRST CONGREGATIONAL CHUCH OF PESCODERO. It was built in 1867 and is the oldest church building on its original site within the San Mateo-Santa Clara County region. A marker is at San Gregorio St., Pescadero.

No. 955: MENLO PARK RAILROAD STATION. The San Francisco and San Jose Railroad Company is the oldest railroad passenger station in California. A marker is at 1100 Merrill Ave.., Menlo Park.

Santa Barbara County

No. 248: GAVIOTA PASS. Here, on Christmas Day, 1846, natives and soldiers from the Presidio of Santa Barbara lay in ambush for Lieutenant Colonel John C. Fremont. Fremont learned of the plot and guided by Benjamin Foxen and his son William, came instead over the San Marcos Pass to capture Santa Barbara without bloodshed. A marker is on State Hwy 101 rest stop, Gaviota.

No. 305: MISSION SANTA INES. It was founded in 1804 by Father Estevan Tapis to reach the Indians living east of the Coast Range. A marker is at 1760 Mission Dr., Solvang.

No. 306: BURTON MOUND. This was thought to be an Indian village of Syujtun. Don Luis Burton acquired the property in 1769. A marker is at 129 W. Mason St., Santa Barbara.

No. 307: CASA DE LA GUERRA. The City of Santa Barbara held its first official meeting here in 1875. A marker is at El Paseo Plaza, Santa Barbara.

No. 308: COVARRUBIAS ADOBE. This adobe was built by Indian labor in 1817 for Don Domingo Carrillo. His daughter married Don Jose Maria Covrrubias in 1838. A marker is at 715 Santa Barbara St., Santa Barbara.

No. 309: MISSION SANTA BARBARA. It was founded in 1786. A Spanish grist mill, sections of aqueducts, and two reservoirs are used today. A marker is at 2201 Laguna St., Santa Barbara.

No.340: MISSION LA PURISIMA. This mission was badly damaged by an earthquake in 1812. It was removed from control of the Franciscans during secularization in 1834. A marker is on State Highway 246, Lompoc.

No. 361: OLD LOBERO THEATRE. Jose Lobero opened the region's first legitimate theatre here on February 22, 1873. A marker is at 33 E Canon Perdido St., Santa Barbara.

No. 535: CARPINTERIA AND INDIAN VILLAGE OF MISHOPSHNOW. The Chumash Indian Village of Mishopshnow was discovered by Juan Rodriguez Cabrillo on August 14, 1542. Portolo's soldiers observing the Indians building wooden canoes, called the village Carpenteria (Carpenter's Shop). A marker is at Carpenteria Valley Museum, 1,000 Carpenteria Ave., Carpenteria.

No. 559: HASTINGS ADOBE. It was built by Captain Horatio Gates Trussell. The adobe is partly constructed of material from the wreck of the old *Winfield Scott* which ran aground on Anacapa Island. A marker is at 412 W. Montecito St., Santa Barbara.

No. 582: WELL, HILL 4. This well was the first well in which a water shutoff was attained by pumping cement through the tubing and back of the casing. A marker is at Rucker Rd., Lompoc.

No. 636: ROYAL SPANISH PRESIDIO. This presidio was built to benefit inhabitants of the Santa Barbara Channel region in 1782. A marker is at Santa Barbara and Canyon Perdido Sts., Santa Barbara.

No. 721: CARRILLO ADOBE. It was built in 1825 by Daniel Hill for his bride. She was the granddaughter of Jose Francisco Ortega, founder and first commandante of the Royal Presidio of Santa Barbara. A marker is at 11 E Carrillo St., Santa Barbara.

No. 877: CHAPEL OF SAN RAMON. It was built by Frederick and Ramona Foxen Wickenden in 1875. A marker is at Repusquet and Foxen Canyon Rd., Santa Maria.

No. 928: SITE OF ORIGINAL MISSION AND REMAINING RUINS OF BUILDINGS OF MISSION CONCEPTION DE MARIA SANTISIMA. The ruins at this site are part of the original Mission La Purisima. A marker is at 5085 T Street, Lompoc.

No. 1037: SANTA BARBARA COUNTY COURTHOUSE. It was constructed in 1929 and is a complex of four buildings occupying an entire city block in downtown Santa Barbara. A marker is on 1100 Anacapa Street, Santa Barbara.

Santa Clara County

No. 249: OLD ADOBE WOMAN'S CLUB. This adobe was among the oldest in Santa Clara Valley. It was one of several rows of homes built in 1792-1800. See the marker at 3260 The Alameda, Santa Clara.

No. 250: OLD SITES OF MISSION SANTA CLARA DE ASIS AND OLD SPANISH BRIDGE. The first mission in this valley was Mission Santa Clara de Thamien. It was built in 1877. A marker is located at Central Expressway and De la Cruz Blvd., Santa Clara.

No. 259: VASQUEZ TREE AND SITE OF 21-MILE HOUSE. This famous tavern and stage stop was located 21 miles from San Jose. The 21-Mile-House was built under a spreading oak that was later called the Vasquez Tree. A marker is at Tennant Ave. and Monterey Hwy., Morgan Hill.

No. 260: SANTA CLARA CAMPAIGN TREATY SITE. Marine Captain Ward Marston and Francisco Sanchez agreed to a treaty to recognize Californians and end seizure of their property. A marker is at Civic Center Park, Santa Clara.

No. 338: MISSION SANTA CLARA. This is the first California Mission to honor a woman, Clare of Assissi. A marker is in front of Mission Church, University of Santa Clara.

No. 339: NEW ALAMDEN MINE. The Indians used pigment from this cinnabar hill for paint. Mercury was mined here as early as 1845. Marker is on Hwy 101, San Jose.

No. 339-1: NEW ALMADEN MINE. Luis Cabolla and Antonio Sunol mined the New Almaden ore in their arrastra. It produced more than a million flasks of quicksilver. A marker is at Bulmore Park, New Almaden.

No. 416: EDWIN MARKHAM HOME. Markham was the author of "Man with the Hoe". He taught school in many places. A marker is at 1600 Senter Rd., San Jose.

No. 417: FIRST NORMAL SCHOOL IN CALIFORNIA (SAN JOSE STATE COLLEGE). It was founded as a private institution, 'Minns' Evening Normal School. It was destroyed by fire in 1880 and heavily damaged by the 1906 earthquake. A marker can be seen at San Carlos and Fourth Streets, San Jose.

No. 433: FIRST SITE OF EL PUEBLO DE SAN JOSE DE GUADALUPE. Lieutenant Jose Joaquin Moraga arrived in the Santa Clara Valley with 14 settlers and their families on November 29, 1777. He founded El Pueblo de San Jose. A marker is in the front parking lot planter, 151 W. Mission St., San Jose.

No. 434: SITE OF CITY GARDENS-NURSERY OF LOUIS PELLIER. Louis Pellier was the founder of California's prune industry. A marker is in the 100 block of W. St. James St., San Jose.

No. 435: SARATOGA. Lumbering in the mountains began in 1847 and brought the area's first settlers in 1850. A marker is located in park at Hwys 9 and 85.

No. 447: GUBSERVILLE: Frank Gubser was a German immigrant and barber. Gubserville was an important stage, mail and teamster stop on the road between San Jose and Saratoga. A marker is at 1481 Saratoga Ave. San Jose.

No. 448: PATCHEN. "Mountain Charley" McKiernan was one of the earliest residents of the Santa Cruz Mountains in 1850. The Patchen Post Office was named for a famous racehorse. A marker is on Old Santa Cruz Hwy and Mtn. Charlie Rd., Holy City.

No. 458: FORBES FLOUR MILL. Not much remains of this four-story stone flour mill. A marker is at Forbes Mill Museum, 75 Church St., Los Gatos.

No. 461: SITE OF CALIFORNIA'S FIRST STATE CAPITOL. California's first state capitol was located directly opposite this tablet marker at City Park Plaza, S. Market St., San Jose.

No. 489: MORELAND SCHOOL. Moreland School was established in 1851 as a subscription school meeting in private homes. A marker is at 4335 Payne Ave. at Saratoga, San Jose.

No. 505: ALMADEN VINEYARDS. Charles La Franc made the first commercial planting of fine European grapes in Santa Clara County to found Almaden Vineyards. A marker is at 1530 Blossom Hill Rd., San Jose.

No. 524: SITE OF JUANA BRIONES DE MIRANDA HOME ON RANCHO LA PURISIMA CONCEPCION. In 1843 Apolinario Miranda, husband of Juana Briones de Miranda, was sent before the subprefect for not living harmoniously with his wife. Shortly after, Juana and her seven children arrived at Rancho la Purisma Concepcion. In 1856, the property was duly confirmed to her. Marker is at 4157 Old Adobe Rd., Palo Alto.

No. 644: MARTIN MURPHY HOME AND ESTATE. Arriving in California in 1844 with his wife and family, Martin Murphy founded Sunnyvale. He constructed a prefabricated house with lumber brought around the HORN. A marker is in the Martin Murphy, Jr., Historical Park, Sunnyvale.

No. 733: PAUL MASSON MOUNTAIN WINERY. This winery has continuously produced wines and champagne since it opened in 1852. A marker is located off State Hwy 9.

No. 800: ARROYO DE SAN JOSEPH CUPERTINO. This arroyo honors San Joseph, patron saint of flight and students. A marker is aat Monta Vista High School, Cupertino.

No. 813: MONTGOMERY HILL. This is where Joseph Montgomery demonstrated aero-dynamic developments indispensable to modern aircraft. A marker is at the entrance to Evergreen College, San Jose.

No. 834: EADWEARD MUYBRIDGE AND THE DEVELOPMENT OF MOTION PICTURES. He conducted motion picture research at the Palo Alto Stock Farm, which is now Stanford University. A marker exists at Stanford University, Palo Alto.

No. 836: PIONEER ELECTRONICS RESEARCH LABORATORY. This was the original laboratory of the Federal Telegraph Company. This is where the three-element radio vacuum tube was invented. Marker is in sidewalk, Channing Ave. and Emerson St., Palo Alto.

No. 854: OLD POST OFFICE. Built in 1892, this was the first federal building in San Jose. A marker is at 110 S. Market, San Jose.

No. 857: JOHN ADAMS SQUIRE HOUSE. This house is a notable example of California's interpretation of the Greco-Roman Classic Revival movement in America. Marker is at 900 University Ave. Palo Alto.

No. 866: LUIS MARIA PERALTA ADOBE. It is believed that this adobe was built before 1800. A marker is located at 184 W. St. John St., San Jose.

No. 868: WINCHESTER HOUSE. This house was built by Sarah Winchester, widow of rifle manufacturer William Winchester. A marker is located at 525 S. Winchester Blvd., San Jose.

No. 888: HAYES MANSION. The Hayes Brothers were early publishers of the San Jose Mercury newspaper. The mansion consists of 62 rooms, 11 fireplaces and was paneled in more than a dozen different woods. A marker is at 200 Edenvale Ave., San Jose.

No. 895: HOSTESS HOUSE. It was designed for the YMCA to serve Camp Fremont as a place for servicemen and visitors. A marker is at 27 Mitchell Lane, Palo Alto.

No. 898: ROBERTO-SUNOL ADOBE. This historic adobe was built in 1836. Antonio Sunol added a second story. A marker is at 770 Lincoln Ave., San Jose.

No. 902: FIRST UNITARIAN CHURCH OF SAN JOSE. It is one of the few churches patterned after the traditional Unitarian churches of Transylvania. A marker is at 160 N. Third St., San Jose.

No. 903: KOTANI-EN. This is a classical Japanese residence in the formal style of a 13th century estate with the roofed walls surrounding a tea house, shrine, gardens and pond. A marker is at 15891 Ravine Rd., Los Gatos.

No. 904: CHARLES COPELAND MORSE RESIDENCE. Morse was a pioneer in the seed industry. A marker is at 981 Fremont St., Santa Clara.

No. 910: ST. JOSEPH'S CATHOLIC CHURCH. It was the first non-mission church in a Spanish California settlement. It was built in 1803. A marker is at 90 S. Market St., San Jose.

No. 913: LOU HENRY HOOVER HOUSE. It was maintained as the Hoover home from 1920 to 1944. A plaque is at 623 Mirada Rd., Stanford University.

No. 945: FIRST SUCCESSFUL INTRODUCTION OF THE HONEYBEE IN CALIFORNIA. On the 1,939-acre Rancho Potrero de Santa Clara, Christopher A. Shelton introduced the honeybee to California. A marker is located at the San Jose Municipal Airport.

No. 952: SITE OF WORLD'S FIRST BROADCASTING STATION. Charles D. Herrold established Station FN, the first radio broadcasting station in the world. Marker is at First and San Fernando Sts., San Jose.

No. 976: INVENTION OF THE FIRST PRACTICABLE INTEGRATED CIRCUIT. Dr. Robert Noyce invented the first integrated circuit that could be produced commercially. A marker is 844 E. Charleston Road, Palo Alto.

No. 1017: GILROY YAMATO HOT SPRINGS RESORT. Gilroy Hot Springs was a popular health and family resort centered on a single hot mineral spring. A marker can be found at New Ave and Roop Road, Gilroy.

Santa Cruz County

No. 342: SITE OF MISSION SANTA CRUZ. Mission la Exaltacion de la Santa Cruz is the 12th mission in the chain of California missions. A marker is located at Plaza Park, Santa Cruz.

No. 449: GLENWOOD. This historic town was founded by Charles C. Martin, who came around the Horn with his wife. Martin homesteaded the area and built a tollgate and station for stagecoaches crossing the mountains. A marker is at 4171 Glenwood Dr., Scott's Valley.

No. 469: VILLA DE BRANCIFORTE. It was founded by Governor Diego de Borica of California on orders of from Spain. A marker is at the corner of Water and Branciforte, Santa Crus.

No. 583: FELTON COVERED BRIDGE. It was believed to be the tallest covered bridge in the country. It stood as the only entry to Felton. A marker is at Covered Bridge Road and Graham Hill Road., Felton.

No. 827: BIG BASIN REDWOODS STATE PARK. A group of conservationists camped at the base of Slippery Rock on May 15, 1900. They formed the Sempervirens Club to preserve the redwoods of Big Basin. A plaque is at State Highway 236, Big Basin.

No. 860: SUPERINTENDENTS OFFICE. This building is Capitola's oldest commercial structure. A marker is at 201 Monterey St., Capitola.

No. 983: SANTA CRUZ BEACH BOARDWALK. This boardwalk was one of the first amusement parks in California. A marker is at 400 Beach St., Santa Cruz.

No. 998: RANCHO SAN ANDRES CASTRO ADOBE. The Castro Adobe functioned as a regional social center. The Castro Family Empire reached across seven land grants to include more than a quarter million acres. A Marker is 184 Old Adobe Road, Watsonville.

Shasta County

No. 10: READING ADOBE. This was the home of Pierson Barton Reading who was a major in Fremont's California Battalion. A marker is at 213 Adobe Rd., Cottonwood.

No. 11: NOBLE PASS ROUTE. William H. Noble showed the route for a wagon road across the Sierra in 1852. A marker is Lassen Volcanic National Park.

No. 32: READING'S BAR. This is where Major Pierson B. Reading and his Indian employees washed out the first gold in Shasta County. A marker is on Clear Creek Road, Redding.

No. 33: SOUTHERN'S STAGE STATION. During a half-century many noted people who made early California history were entertained in this hotel. A marker is on old Highway 99, Castella.

No. 58: OLD CALIFORNIA-OREGON ROAD. This was a main artery of travel by pioneers between Trinity River and the northern mines. A marker is on Highway 99, Anderson.

No. 77: OLD TOWN OF SHASTA. It was once called Reading Springs. It was renamed in 1850. A marker is at Shasta State Historic Park, Shasta.

No. 78: CLEAR CREEK. Near here is where Major Pierson Reading found gold in 1848. A marker is on Old Highway 99 and Canyon Rd., Redding.

No. 116: BATTLE ROCK. The "Battle of the Crags" was fought here in 1885. This was a conflict between Modoc Indians and the settlers. The war was about the gold miners destroying the native fishing waters in the lower Soda Springs area. A marker can be found at the entrance of Castle Crags State Park.

No. 120: DERSCH HOMESTEAD. George and Anna Maria Dersch took up a homestead in 1861. There was trouble between the Indians and the settlers. The Indians raided the Dersch Ranch and killed Mrs. Dersch. A marker is on Dersch Rd. at Bear Creek, Anderson.

No. 131: WHISKEYTOWN. It was first called Whiskey Creek for the stream on which it was located. The town's name was changed to Whiskeytown. A marker is at the intersection of Whiskey Creek Road and State Highway 299.

No. 148: BASS HILL. This was a favorite hold-up spot in stagecoach days. A marker has been placed there in memory of W.L. Smith, division stage agent.

No. 166: FRENCH GULCH. It was founded by French miners in 1849. French Gulch was the trailhead on the western branch of the California-Oregon Trail.

No. 355: FORT CROOK. It was established in 1857 by Lieutenant George Crook for protection of immigrants and settlers. A marker is at the corner of McArthur Rd. and Soldier Mtn. Dr., Glenburn.

No. 377: PIONEER BABY'S GRAVE. Charles, the infant son of George and Helena Cohn Brownstein, of Red Bluff, died December 14, 1864. Since there was no Jewish cemetery in Red Bluff, they made the journey to Shasta bury their baby.

No. 379: FORT READING. This was the first and largest fort in Northern California. It was abandoned in 1867.

No. 483: FATHER RINALDI'S FOUNDATION OF 1856. Father Rinaldi decided to build a church of cut stone to replace the tiny wooden church that had served since1853. A marker is at the intersection of Red Bluff Rd. and Crocker Alley, Shasta.

No. 519: BELL'S BRIDGE. It was built in 1856 by J.J. Bell. It was an important toll bridge on the road from Shasta City to Tehama. A marker is on old Highway 99 and Clear Creek Rd., Redding.

No. 555: LOCKHART FERRY. It was built in 1856 as a link in the first wagon road from Yreka to Red Bluff. A marker is on State Highway 299, at Fall River Mills.

No. 759: SITE OF THE FIRST SCHOOL IN FALL RIVER VALLEY. The windowless building was a log structure that measured 20 feet by 30 feet. A marker is on State Highway 299.

Sierra County

No. 421: HENNESS PASS ROAD. This was the main emigrant trail between Virginia City, Nevada and Marysville. A marker is at the intersection of Ridge and Henness Pass Rds., Alleghany.

No. 695: PLUM VALLEY HOUSE. John Bopp built the Plum Valley House of hewn logs and whip sawn lumber. A marker was on Ridge Rd.

No. 971: SIERRA COUNTY SHERIFF'S GALLOWS. On November 27, 1885, twenty-year old James O'Neill was hanged from this gallows. He had murdered Webber Lake dairyman John Woodward. A marker is at the Sierra County Jail Yard, Downeyville.

Siskiyou County

No. 9: CAPTAIN JACK'S STRONGHOLD. Captain Jack and his Indian forces had successfully resisted U.S. troops from December 1, 1872 until April 18, 1873. A marker is on Highway 139 and County Road 120.

No. 13: GUILLEM'S GRAVEYARD. Almost 100 soldiers were killed during the Modoc Indian War. The bodies were moved to the National Cemetery in Washington, DC. A marker is located in the Lava Beds National Monument.

No. 110: CANBY'S CROSS-1873. General E, R. S. Canby was murdered here in April 1873 while holding a peace parley with Captain Jack and other Indian chiefs. A marker is in Lava Beds National Monument.

No. 317: SITE OF FORT JONES. This site is dedicated to three members of the U.S. Dragoons who became pioneer settlers in the area. A marker is located at E Side Rd and State Highway, Fort Jones.

No. 396: STRAWBERRY VALLEY STAGE STAION. When the business center was moved to its present location on the railroad in 1886, its name was changed to Sisson. In 1923, it was renamed Mount Shasta City. A marker is at W. Jessie St. and Old Stage Road, Mt. Shasta.

No. 517: EMIGRANT TRAIL CROSSING OF PRESENT HIGHWAY. As early as 1852, wagon trains of overland emigrants crossed into Shasta Valley and Yreka. A marker is on State Highway 97, Weed.

No. 901: WEST MINER STREET-THIRD STREET HISTORIC DISTRICT, YREKA. With the discovery of gold in the nearby flats, Yreka became the commercial and transportation hub for the mining camps. A marker is on Miner St. and Broadway.

Solano County

No. 153: BENICIA CAPITOL. This was one of four locations of the State's "Capitol on Wheels" from February 25, 1853 to February 25, 1854. A marker is at First and G streets, Benicia.

No. 174: FIRST BUILDING ERECTED IN CALIFORNIA BY MASONIC LODGE FOR USE AS A HALL. This building served as a Masonic Temple for Benicia Lodge No. 5 until 1888. Marker is at 110 W. J St., Benicia.

No. 175: FIRST PROTESTANT CHURCH. This was the first Protestant church established in California with an ordained pastor. Marker is at 1st and 2nd Sts., Benicia.

No. 176: BENICIA ARSENAL. The arsenal played an important role in crises such as the Indian wars. A marker is at the Main gate, Adams and Jefferson, Sts., Benicia.

No. 177: FORMER BENICIA BARRACKS. The barracks became part of the Benicia Arsenal, which closed in 1964. A marker is at Benicia National Guard Armory, 711 Hillcrest, Benicia.

No. 534: VACA-PENA ADOBE. Governor Pio Pico granted Felipe Pena and Manuel Cabeza Vaca the 10-square-league Rancho Los Putos in 1845. A marker is on Pena Adobe Road, Vacaville.

No. 574: SITE OF STATE CAPITOL AT VALLEJO. Vallejo was the official seat of government from February 4, 1851 to February 4, 1853. A marker is between Sacramento and Santa Clara Streets, Vallejo.

No. 751: FIRST U.S. NAVAL AIR STATION IN THE PACIFIC. Mare Island had the Navy's first shipyard, ammunition depot, hospital, Marine barracks, cemetery, chapel, and radio station in the Pacific. A marker is at Main gate, Mare Island Naval Shipyard, Vallejo.

No. 751: ROCKVILLE STONE CHAPEL. This chapel was erected in 1856 by pioneers of Methodist Episcopal Church South with volunteer labor. A marker is at Rockville Cemetery, Rockville.

No. 795: BENICIA SEMINARY. It was founded in 1852 as the Young Ladies Seminary of Benicia. A marker is at First and Second Sts., Benicia.

No. 804: UNIVESITY OF CALIFORNIA EXPERIMENTAL FARM, WOLFSKILL GRANT. John A. Wolfskill arrived here in 1842 kadeb with fruit seeds and cuttings. He became father of the fruit industry in this region. A marker is at University of California Experimental Farm, Winters.

No. 862: SAINT PAUL'S EPISCOPAL CHURCH. This church was built by shipwrights of the Pacific Mail and Steamship Company. A marker is at 120 E "J" Street, Benicia.

No. 880: FISCHER-HANLON HOUSE. In 1849, Joseph Fischer purchased this lot. He moved the house, which was reputed to be an old hotel, onto it. The building is said to be an outstanding example of East Coast Federalist styling. A marker is at 135 W "G" Street, Benicia.

No. 973: TURNER-ROBERTSON SHIPYARD, 1883-1918. Matthew Turner was the most prodigious shipbuilder in North America. He built 228 vessels. He moved shipyard to Benicia. It was purchased by James Robertson. A marker is at Matthew Turn Shipyard Park, Benicia.

Sonoma County

No. 3: MISSION SAN FRANCISCO SOLANO. The mission became a parish church following secularization in 1834. A marker is at Sonoma State Historic Park.

No. 4: GENERAL M.G. VALLEJO'S HOME. It was called *Lachryma Montis* (Tears of the Mountains). A marker is at Sonoma State Historic Park, Sonoma.

No. 4: FORT ROSS. It was built by the Russians in 1812. When the Russians withdrew to Alaska in 1841, John Sutter bought the improvements and supplies. A marker is at 19005 Coast Highway, Jenner.

No. 7: BEAR FLAG MONUMENT. The Bear Flag was raised to declare California free of Mexican rule. It was brought down when the American flag was raised in Monterey. A marker is in the Sonoma Plaza.

No. 17: BLUE WING INN. It was one of the first hostelries in Northern California. A marker is in Sonoma State Historic Park.

No. 18: PETALUMA ADOBE. This adobe was at the center of General Mariano Guadalupe Vallejo's ranch. A marker is at Petaluma Adobe State Historic Park, Petaluma.

No. 234: LUTHER BURBANK HOME AND GARDEN. Luther Burbank developed some of the world's most treasured fruits and flowers here. A marker is at the 200 block of Santa Rosa Ave., Santa Rosa.

No. 237: TEMELEC HALL. This house was built by Captain Granville P. Swift, a member of the Bear Flag Party. A marker is at Temelec Adult Community, Sonoma.

No. 316: PRESIDIO OF SONOMA (SONOMA BARRACKS). Sonoma Barracks was used as the headquarters of the Bear Flag Revolt. A marker is in Sonoma State Historic Park, Sonoma.

No. 392: BUENA VISTA WINERY AND VINEYARDS. This was the birthplace of California wines. A marker is at 18000 Old Winery Road, Sonoma.

No. 392-1: SITE OF HARASZTHY VILLA. This was built by Count Agoston Haraszthy, "Father of California Viticulture". A marker is at Castle Road, Sonoma.

No. 496: SWISS HOTEL. It was built by Don Salvador Vallejo. It was later used as a hotel and restaurant. A marker is 18 W Spain St., Sonoma.

No. 501: SALVADOR VALLEJO HOUSE. This was the home of Captain Salvador Vallejo, brother of General Mariano Vallejo. A marker is at 421 First St., Sonoma.

No. 621: ITALIAN SWISS COLONY. Italian immigrants established an agricultural colony here in 1881. By 1905, ten gold medals had been awarded wines produced here. A marker is on Asti Post Office Rd., Asti.

No. 627: UNION HOTEL AND UNION HALL. The Union Hotel was conducted as a hotel until 1955, when Bank of America acquired the property. A marker is at 35 Napa and First St., Sonoma.

No. 667: NASH ADOBE. John H. Nash was taken prisoner by Lieutenant William T. Sherman in 1847 for refusing to relinquish his post as alcalde to Lilburn W. Boggs. A marker is at 579 First St., Sonoma.

No. 692: HOOD HOUSE. The property was purchased in 1943 by the California Department of the Youth Authority for Los Guilucos School for Girls. A marker is 7501 Sonoma Highway, Santa Rosa.

No. 739: VINEYARD AND WINERY (SAN FRANCISCO SOLANO MISSION VINEYARD) Much of the original mission vineyard is still planted to choice wine grapes. Marker is at 394 Fourth St., Sonoma.

No. 743: JACK LONDON STATE HISTORIC PARK. Many of the works of renowned author Jack London are housed here. A marker is at Glen Ellen.

No. 820: ST. TERESA'S CHURCH. It was built in 1859 by New England ship carpenters. A marker exists at Bodega Highway, Bodega.

No. 833, BODEGA BAY AND HARBOR. Pioneer ships of many nations used Bodega Bay as an anchorage. A marker is at Doran Park, Bodega Bay.

No. 835: COOPER'S SAWMILL. The mill served as a barrier to Russian encroachment from the West. A marker is located at Mirabel and River Roads, Santa Rosa.

No. 879: COTATI DOWNTOWN PLAZA. Cotati's hexagonal town plan is one of only two in the United States. It was designed by Newton Smyth as an alternative to the traditional grid. A marker is at Old Redwood Highway and E. Cotati Ave., Cotati.

No. 893: WALTERS RANCH HOP KILN. It is a significant example of stone hop kilns in the north coast region. A marker is at 6959 Westside Road, Healdsburg.

No. 915: PETRIFIED FOREST. This is the state's only Petrified Forest dating from the Eocene period. A marker is at 5000 Medica Rd., Santa Rosa.

No. 939: TWENTHIETH CENTURY FOLK ART ENVIRONMENTS JOHN MEDICA GARDENS. John Medica spent 20 years transforming a barren hillside into a magical garden. A marker is at 5000 Medica Road, Santa Rosa.

No. 981: ICARIA-SPERANZA COMMUNE. This was a social experiment in communal living . A marker is on Asti Road, Cloverdale.

Stanislaus County

No. 347: KNIGHT'S FERRY. It was once called Dentville. The rare wooden-covered bridge was designed by U.S. Grant, a brother-in-law of the Dent Brothers. A marker is on Sonora Road, Knights Ferry.

No. 414: LA GRANGE. French settlers established a community here. After destructive floods, citizens of French Bar relocated one mile upstream. The town was renamed La Grange. A marker is at 30173 Yosemite Blvd., La Grange.

No, 415: THE WILLMS RANCH. John R. Willms and John H. Kappelmann engaged in the hotel and butcher business in Buena Vista. They bought up mining claims and settler's claims until they had a tract of 2,600 acres. The KW brand was the first in Tuolumne County. A marker is on Willms Rd., Knights Ferry.

No. 418: EMPIRE CITY. This memorial is dedicated to pioneer men and women of Empire City and vicinity. A marker is on County Highway J-7, Empire

No. 934: TEMPORARY DETENTION CAMP FOR JAPANESE AMERICANS-TURLOCK ASSEMBLY CENTER. People of Japanese ancestry were held here during World War II. A marker is Stanislaus Fairground.

Sutter County

No. 346: HOCK FARM. John Sutter got Fort Ross and Hock Farm from the Russians. The fort and farm buildings were located on the banks of the Feather River. A plaque is on Messick Road, five miles south of Yuba City.

No. 929. SITE WHERE THOMPSON SEEDLESS GRAPES WERE PROPAGATED. William Thompson was an Englishman who settled here with his family in 1863. He sent to New York for three cuttings called Lady de Coverly. Only one cutting survived. It became known as Thompson's seedless grape. A marker is at 9001, Colusa Way, Yuba City.

Tehama County

No. 12: GENERAL WILLIAM B. IDE RESIDENCE. He helped organize the Bear Flag Revolt. A marker is at William B. Ide Adobe State Historic Park, Red Bluff.

No. 117: HOME OF MRS. JOHN BROWN. Mrs. John Brown was the widow of the famous abolitionist, John Brown, of Harper's Ferry. A marker is 135 Main St., Red Bluff.

No . 183: FIRST TEHAMA COUNTY COURTHOUSE. Tehama County's Board of Supervisors met in the Union Hotel. The courthouse is now on property that is part of an original land grant to Robert Hasty Thomes. A marker is at intersection of Second and D Streets, Tehama.

No. 357: INDIAN MILITARY POST OF NOMI LACKEE INDIAN RESERVATION. The Nomi Lackee Indian Reservation controlled 300 to 2,500 militant Indians. A marker is on Osborn Road, Flournoy.

Trinity County

No. 709: WEAVERVILLE JOSS HOUSE. Hundreds of Chinese miners came to Weaverville in the 1850s and prospered despite hardships, discrimination and a tax on foreign miners. A marker is located on State Highway 299 and Oregon St., Weaverville.

No. 788: LAA GRANGE MINE. This mine was originally known as the Oregon Mountain Group of Claims. Large-scale operations ceased in 1918. A marker is at State Highway 299, Weaverville.

Tulare County

No. 388: FIRST TULE RIVER INDIAN RESERVATION. The reservation was established in 1857. A marker is located at Alta Vista School, Porterville.

No. 389: KAWEAH POST OFFICE. The Kaweah cooperative colony was a utopian project started in 1886. A marker is at 43795 N. Fork Dr., Kaweah.

No. 410: CHARTER OAK ELECTION TREE. Under this tree on July 19, 1852, Major James D. Savage conducted an election by which Tulare County was organized. A marker is on Charter Oak Dr., Visalia.

No. 413: TAILHOLT. Tailholt began as a gold mining camp. Its name was changed to White River about 1870. A marker is on County Highway M109 and County Hwy M12.

No. 471: BUTTERFIELD STAGE ROUTE. This route was laid out as the Stockton-Los Angeles Road. A marker exists at Hermosa Street and State Highway 65, Lindsay.

No. 473: TULE RIVER STAGE STATION. Peter Goodhue operated an emigrant trail stopping place on the bank of the Tule River, until the river change its course. A marker is at Porterville Public Park.

No. 648: FOUNTAIN SPRINGS. This was on the road to the Kern River gold fields. See the marker at County Rds. J22 and M109, Fountain Springs.

No. 934: TEMPORARY DETENTION CAMP FOR JAPANESE AMERICANS-TULARE ASSEMBLY CENTER. Persons of Japanese ancestry were held here during World War II. A marker is located at the Tulare County Fairgrounds, Tulare.

Tuolumne County

No. 122: MONTEZUMA. A first record of Montezuma was June 8, 1850, when partners Solomon Miller and Peter K. Aurand were attacked. Aurand was killed. The killers were a group of Mexicans during the foreign miner's tax. A marker is on State Highway 49.

No. 123: COLUMBIA. It was called "Gem of the Southern Mines". A marker is located at Columbia State Historic Park, Columbia.

No. 124: TUTTLETOWN. It was named for Judge Anson A.H. Tuttle, who built the first log cabin here in 1848. A marker is on State Highway 49, at Wilcox Ranch Road, Tuttletown.

No. 138: MARK TWAIN CABIN. This is a replica of Mark Twain's cabin with the original chimney and fireplace. It's located on Jackass Hill off Highway 49.

No. 139: ST. JAMES EPISCOPAL CHURCH. St. James is the oldest Episcopal Church building in the state. A marker is located at N. Washington, State Highway 49, Sonora.

No. 140: WELLS FARGO EXPRESS BUILDING. It was built in 1849. A marker is at corner of Main Street and Solinsky Alley, Chinese Camp.

No. 395: SHAW'S FLAT. Among the famous at this mining community was James D. Fair, for whom the Fairmont Hotel in San Francis is named. Another favorite story is about the bartender who added to his income by panning the gold dust tropped on his muddy boots as he served his customers. You'll find a marker at Shaw's Flat Road and Mt. Brow Road, Columbia.

No. 406: BIG OAK FLAT. It was first called Savage Diggins when gold was first discovered there. It was renamed for the giant oak tree that stood in the middle of town. A marker is on Highway 129 at Big Oak Flat.

No. 407: SUMMERSVILLE (TUOLUMNE). The town was first called Eureka, then called Summersville, then called Carters, and finally named Tuolumne. A marker is in an island on Carter St., Tuolumne.

No. 419: JACKSONVILLE. Jacksonville is now under the waters of Don Pedro Reservoir. A markere is at Vista Point at the approach of Don Pedro Bridge.

No. 420: SOULSBYVILLE. This is the first community to be founded in Tuolumne County. A marker is located on the corner of Soulsbyville Rd. and Community Dr., Soulsbyville.

No. 422: SONORA-MONO ROAD: Jedediah Smith is said to be the first white man to cross Sonora Pass in 1827. A marker is on State Highway 108, at Sugar Pine.

No. 423: CHINESE CAMP. The first Chinese tong war in the state was held here. It was between the Sam Yap and the Yan Woo Tongs. A marker is located at State Highway 120 and Main St., Chinese Camp.

No. 424: SAWMILL FLAT. Two sawmills were erected her in the 1850s. The legendary "Battle of Sawmill Flat" would have taken place here. A marker is at 22041 Sawmill Flat Road, Columbia.

No. 431: JAMESTOWN. The town became known as the "Gateway to the Mother Lode". A marker is on Main and Donovan Sts., Jamestown.

No. 432: SPRINGFIELD. It got its name from the abundant springs gushing from limestone boulders. A marker is at the intersection of Springfield and Horseshoe Bend Rds., Columbia.

No. 438: PARROTT'S FERRY. This ferry was in operation until 1903. A marker is on the Calaveras side of the Columbia-Vallecito Highway Bridge.

No. 445: CHEROKEE. Gold was discovered here by the Scott brothers, who were descendants of Cherokee Indians. A marker is on Confidence-Tuolumne City Road, Tuolumne City.

No. 446: GROVELAND. It was formerly called "First Garrote" because of the hanging of a Mexican for the stealing of a horse. A marker is on the corner of Main and Back Streets, Groveland.

No. 460: SECOND GARROTE. The famous hangman's tree, part of which still stands (1950), is reported to have been used to hang a number of lawbreakers. A marker is on State Highway 120, Groveland.

Ventura County

No. 113: JUNIPERO SERRA'S CROSS. Junipero Serra erected a cross, known as *La Loma de la Cruz* or the Hill of the Cross, founding Mission San Buenaventura March 31, 1782. This was the ninth and last mission founded by Father Serra. A marker is in Grant Park, Ventura.

No. 114: OLD MISSION RESERVOIR. This was a settling tank from which water was distributed to the church. A marker is located in Eastwood Park, Ventura.

No. 114-1: SAN BUENAVENTURA MISSION AQUEDUCT. The aqueduct was built by Chumash Indians. A marker is located at 234 Canada Large Rd., Ventura.

No. 115: OLIVAS ADOBE. It's the only two-story adobe in the Santa Clara Valley. A marker is at 4200 Olivas Park, Ventura.

No. 310: MISSION SAN BUENAVENTURA. The mission was established in 1782. A marker is at 210 E. Main St., Ventura.

No. 553: RANCHO CAMULOS. Governor Juan Alvarado granted this 48,815-acre Rancho San Francisco to Antonio Del Valle. A marker is at State Highway 126, Piru.

No. 624: WARRING PARK. Portola discovered this populace village of Piru Indians here. A marker can be seen at Warring Park, Piru.

No. 659: STAGECOACH INN. It was built in 1876. The lumber came by sea and was freighted up the steep Conejo Grade by multi-team wagons. A marker is at 51 South Ventu Park Rd., Newbury Park.

Ho. 727: PORTOLA EXPEDITONL. The Portola Expedition arrived at Arroyo Mupu and Santa Paula Creek. A marker exists at Santa Paula Boys Club Recreation Center.

No. 756: SYCAMORE TREE. This tree has been used as a resting place, a polling place, a temporary post office, and an outdoor chapel. A marker is on Highway 126, Santa Paula.

No. 847: VENTURA COUNTY COURTHOUSE. The courthouse was designed by Albert C. Martin and dedicated in 1913. Martin was considered an early pioneer of architecture. A marker can be seen at 501 Poli Street, Ventura.

No. 939: TWENTIETH CENTURY FOLK ART-GRANDMA PRISBREY'S BOTTLE VILLAGE. Tressa Prisbey, nearly 60-years-old, began building a fanciful village of shrines, walkways and sculpture. See the marker at 4595 Cochran St., Simi Valley.

No. 979: RANCHO SIMI. This was the headquarters of the Spanish *Rancho San Jose de Nuestra Senora de Altagarcia y Simi.* A marker is at Robert P. Strathearn Historical Park, Simi Valley.

No. 996: UNION OIL COMPANY BUILDING. The Santa Paula Hardware Company Building was more commonly referred to as the Union Oil Building. A marker can be found at 1003 E. Main, Santa Paula.

Yolo County

No. 851: WOODLAND OPERA HOUSE. It was the first opera house to serve the Sacramento Valley. A marker was placed between Main St. and Dead Cat Alley, Woodland.

No. 864: GABLE MANSION. The structure was built in 1885 for Amos and Harvey Gable, pioneer Yolo County ranchers. A marker is at 659 First St., Woodland.

No. 1040: FIRST PACIFIC COAST SALMON CANNERY. This small canning operation was the beginning of the West Coast's salmon canning industry. A marker is on the Sacramento River, foot of K Street.

Yuba County

No. 320: TIMBUCTOO. It was once the largest town in Yuba County. At its height, it had a church, theatre, stores, hotels, saloons and a Wells Fargo office. A marker is on State Highway 20 on Timbuctoo Road, Smartsville.

No. 321: SMARTSVILLE. One of the prominent features of the town today is its churches. A marker is on State Highway 20, Smartsville.

No 493: JOHNSON'S RANCH. It was the first settlement reached by emigrants traveling by wagon train using the Emigrant Donner Trail. A marker is at Tomita Park, Fourth and Main Sts., Wheatland.

No. 799-3: OVERLAND EMIGRANT TRAIL. It was used by pioneers, mines, trappers, herdsmen and adventurers. Rescuers of the Donner Party assembled here. A marker is on Spencerville Road, Wheatland.

No. 934: TEMPORARY DETENTION CAMP FOR JAPANESE AMERICANS-MARYSVILLE ASSEMBLY CENTER. People of Japanese ancestry were held at these centers during World War II. A marker is at Arboga Community, Arboga Road.

No. 1003: WHEATLAND HOP RIOT OF 1913. This riot was a bloody clash at the Durst Ranch. It climaxed the growing tensions of farm workers and resulted in four deaths and many injuries. A marker is at intersection of South A Street and 6th Street, Wheatland.

Meet the Author

Alton Pryor

Alton Pryor has published fifty-plus books since turning 70 in 1997—many of them about California's past and the colorful characters who rode our trails to fame or infamy.

To date he has sold more than 450,000-plus copies of his first book, "Little Known Tales in California History", and has done respectably well with his other titles.

But until fate derailed his 33-year journalism career, he never aspired to write a book, and certainly never anticipated he would come to be regarded as "Mr. Self-Publishing" by his peers in the Sacramento area. "I would have liked living in the Old West," he says. "I wanted, at one time, to be a really good cowboy. I had horses as a young man and once took a raw colt and trained it to work cattle."

But, by the time Pryor was born on March 19, 1927, the era of gunslingers and gold miners was over, and he started life, instead, on his family's farm outside of King City in the Salinas Valley.

He was terminated after writing for 27 years for California Farmer Magazine. The magazine was sold to a Midwest firm.

Pryor turned to writing books and says now, "I wish I had been fired 20 years earlier."

Index

Made in the USA
San Bernardino, CA
18 March 2019